IRISH
BIBLICAL
APOCRYPHA

IRISH
BIBLICAL
APOCRYPHA

SELECTED TEXTS IN TRANSLATION

edited
by
Máire Herbert
and
Martin McNamara MSC

T & T CLARK
EDINBURGH

First Published 1989

ISBN 0 567 09524 X

British Library Cataloguing in Publication Data

Herbert, Máire
Irish Biblical Apocrypha.
1. Bible. Apocryphal books. Irish versions
I. Title   II. McNamara, Martin
229' .05'9162

Printed and bound in Great Britain by Billing & Sons Ltd, Worcester.

Dedicated to the memory of
St. John D. Seymour,
Montague Rhodes James
and to other pioneers in the study of the
Irish Biblical Apocrypha.

ACKNOWLEDGMENTS

The editors and publishers gratefully acknowledge the financial support of the Irish Biblical Association in the preparation and publication of this work.

The editors and publishers would like to acknowledge their indebtedness to Michael Gordon and Donal Kingston of Computer Bureau University College Cork for technical assistance, and to Peter Moreau of Laser Graphics, 8 Merrion Square, Dublin 2, for production of camera ready copy.

CONTENTS

PREFACE

Professor J. H. Charlesworth

In the present decade, in the eighties, New Testament scholars throughout the world have highlighted the central significance of the documents usually relegated to church historians and categorized as New Testament Apocrypha. The renewed interest in the Jesus of history (Jesus research), the re-examination of the history of the synoptic tradition, the fuller exploration of the transmission of the sayings of Jesus, and the search for pre-70 gospel traditions have all been enriched by a study of the New Testament Apocrypha. Singularly important is certainly the Gospel of Thomas. The renewed interest in the Apocrypha is placarded by the fact that R. E. Brown, in his presidential address to the *Studiorum Novi Testamenti Societas*, felt compelled to focus on "The Gospel of Peter and Canonical Gospel Priority" (*NTS* 33 [1988] 321-343).

In *Rechtgläubigkeit und Ketzerei im ältesten Christentum* (BHT 10; Tübingen, 1934, 1964 [2d. ed]; ET in 1971) W. Bauer showed that "heresy" does not always postdate "orthodoxy". In his introduction to the New Testament H. Koester endeavours to free the New Testament documents from the canon of the Church and to place them in their historical settings, among other gospels, acts, letters, and apocalypses. In "Is the New Testament a Field of Study?" (*Second Century* 1 [1981] 19-35) L. E. Keck warns us that the New Testament is not an isolated field of research. In order to understand the documents later collected into the canon of the New Testament we must ask what the authors intended to say to whom, who was reading them, and how were they being interpreted. We must also seek to comprehend what oral and written sources were available to the intracanonical authors, why they choose and stressed some over others, and what writings or traditions they were reacting against. It is now universally recognised that such concerns thrust us deep into a study of extracanonical documents, some of which may contain redacted traditions that even antedate the composition of the earliest canonical gospel.

In the past our work on the Apocrypha has been guided by the classics: by Fabricius, Migne, James, and Hennecke-Schneemelcher-Wilson. Now we can benefit from the magisterial collections by M. Erbetta, *Gli Apocrifi del Nuovo Testamento* (1966-1975), and by L. Moraldi, *Apocrifi del Nuovo Testamento* (1971). In the early eighties L'Association pour l'Etude de la Littérature Apocryphe Chrétienne, under the presidency of F. Bovon, launched a project to publish the "Christian Apocryphal Literature" in the *Series Apocryphorum*, under the *Corpus Christianorum*.

The Corpus Apocryphorum Hiberniae is organized by some distinguished and revered specialists, including Father Martin McNamara, MSC. I am pleased to have played a small part in encouraging this project. Some Apocrypha are preserved only in Old Irish and important recensions of others are preserved in this language. We know of the early connection between Ireland and the Orient. To focus research on the Apocrypha Hiberniae is to bring into view the milieu of Old Ireland, its links with the Holy Land, and the complex and creative traditions that enlivened the earliest Christians who endeavoured to imagine the lives of Jesus, his family, and his earliest followers.

J. H. Charlesworth
George L. Collord Professor of New Testament Language
and Literature,
Princeton Theological Seminary,
Princeton, N.J.,
14 March 1989.

INTRODUCTION

Martin McNamara, MSC

1. History of Research

We are currently experiencing a more than ordinary interest in the Apocrypha of the New Testament and in both the Apocrypha and Pseudepigrapha of the Old. Evidence of this can be seen in such recent collections of translations as *The Old Testament Pseudepigrapha* (2 volumes; 1983, 1984)[1] edited by Professor James H. Charlesworth and in *The Apocryphal Old Testament* (1984) edited by H. F. Sparks[2]. It is also clear from the critical edition of the New Testament Apocrypha, accompanied by translations, being prepared by the Association pour l'Étude de la Littérature Apocryphe Chrétienne (AELAC) and being published in the *Series Apocryphorum* of the *Corpus Christianorum*. Translations of the Apocrypha have also recently been published, or are currently being made, in modern languages such as Dutch, German, Italian, Japanese and Spanish.

It is only in relatively recent times that the rich Irish tradition in apocryphal literature has become more widely known and appreciated. Much of this Irish material is in the Irish language (Gaelic). It is not that the individual items have not been studied and published by scholars of Gaelic. Quite the contrary, in fact. The greater part of them have been edited from the manuscripts from the latter part of the last century onwards, often with translations into English, German or French. This work, however, has been published in periodicals principally dedicated to the study of the Celtic languages and literatures such as *Ériu, Revue Celtique, Zeitschrift für celtische Philologie*, journals not easily accessible to students interested in the Apocrypha. A factor partly explaining the general neglect of the material may have been the tendency of Celtic scholars to approach their treatment of the items from the linguistic standpoint, and as individual pieces, rather than as so many witnesses to an Apocrypha tradition much larger than Irish or the Celtic countries.

M.R. James paid attention to some of the Irish evidence on the Apocrypha in essays in *The Journal of Theological Studies* in 1909/10 and 1918/19 and in other studies besides[3]. The most significant early contribution in the field was made by St. John D. Seymour in a series of studies during the 1920s[4], culminating in his book *Irish Visions of the Other-World: a Contribution to the Study of Mediaeval Visions*[5] in 1930. Among his more significant contributions was an essay in 1923 on "The Irish Versions of the *Transitus Mariae*"[6] in which he gives what he himself describes as "a fairly full résumé" of the form of this apocryphal writing as found in *Liber Flavus Fergusiorum* of the Royal Irish Academy, Dublin (MS 23 O 48). Both Seymour and James repeatedly commented on the relationships between Irish apocryphal literature and that of the East, in particular with the Apocrypha of the Syrian Church.

In 1937 R. Willard took up Seymour's "fairly full résumé" of the *Liber Flavus* text of the *Transitus Mariae*[7]. He agrees with Seymour and James regarding its close connection with the Syriac form of the apocryphon, and comments on its value: "There can be no doubt that in the final evaluation of the Apocrypha relative to the Dormition and Assumption, the Irish must play an important part"[8]. In a footnote he says: "It is to be hoped that we may have soon an adequate edition, with full editorial apparatus and translation"[9]. The first full translation of this important *Liber Flavus* text is given below.

A few years later other texts on the Assumption of the Virgin were published by Charles Donahue, together with an examination of the Irish tradition of the *Dormitio*[10], i.e. an edition of the Irish text of Oxford, Bodleian, MS Laud Misc. 610, fol. 34-38, together with translation, and cognate Latin text of Trinity College, Dublin, MS F.5.3, pp. 143-144.

The importance of the Irish evidence for the full understanding of the *Transitus Mariae* was again stressed by Victor Arras in his edition and study of the Ethiopic text of this apocryphon[11]. He regrets that the edition of the text is extremely rare even in the largest European libraries, and expresses the hope that it will be reprinted. Seymour's view on the close relation of the Irish to the Syriac tradition was a little later reinforced by Michel van Esbroeck, another leading authority on that particular apocryphal writing[12].

A major work, showing the importance of the Irish evidence for a study of the Apocrypha, was published in 1952 by Dr William W. Heist, *The Fifteen Signs before Doomsday*[13]. In 1954 Professor Bernhard Bischoff published his seminal essay on   Irish exegetes and exegesis between A.D. 650 and 800[14]. Most of the thirty-nine writings to which he drew attention were of Irish origin or had Irish connections. A feature of this literature, Bischoff noted, was the presence in it of passages of rare works, not otherwise preserved, including some apocryphal items such as the Gospel according to the Hebrews (or the Gospel of the Nazareans)[15].

Interest in the field of early Irish ecclesiastical learning, and of Irish Apocrypha, gradually increased during the sixties and later. Further items of Irish Apocrypha were being published and studied. The most significant event in this line was the identification by Professor James Carney of an early Irish text (from ca. A.D. 750) of the Infancy Gospel of Thomas in a seventeenth century MS (Dublin, National Library of Ireland G 50). He published a provisional edition of this in 1958 and the definitive edition in 1964[16]. A further major item is the Adam and Eve material in the Irish *Saltair na Rann*, with its rich apocryphal content. The text of this section has been edited with translation by David Greene and Fergus Kelly, with companion volume containing commentary by Brian Murdoch[16a]. The changed scene gradually became reflected in works concerned with the Apocrypha in general. In volume 1 of his monumental *Repertorium biblicum medii aevi* in 1940 Fridericus Stegmüller lists some 210 apocryphal works, and of these only three or four are said to be represented by Irish texts[17]. In the *Supplementum* to this published in vol. VIII (1976) matters improved somewhat, with five entries for the Irish evidence[18]. In 1973 David Dumville published a major essay on biblical Apocrypha in the early Irish Church[19]. He remarks that a remarkable amount of apocryphal material was demonstrably known in Ireland during the Old-Irish period (i.e. prior to A.D. 900). He presents evidence suggesting that Spain may have been an important immediate source for such literature, especially during the seventh century when contacts between the two countries seem to have been closest. He believes that there is some ground for a suspicion that in Ireland the Apocrypha benefitted from a greater tolerance than would have been accorded them elsewhere in Western Europe[20]. In 1975 the present writer published an introduction to the subject, together with a list of all the Irish Apocrypha known to him, accompanied by a summary examination of each group and individual item[21]. In his monograph *The Pseudepigrapha and Modern Research*, James H. Charlesworth drew attention to this work and to the rich vernacular Irish literature on the Apocrypha[22]. Later as guest lecturer to the Irish Biblical Association in 1985, Dr Charlesworth encouraged the Association, through its President Professor Seán Freyne and the present writer to form a plan for the publication of the corpus of Irish Apocrypha and promised to give freely of his advice. In 1984 the Irish Biblical Association approved a plan to work towards the publication of these Apocrypha.

In the meantime in Europe (Lausanne-Paris) interested scholars working in the field were laying the foundations of what would become the Association for the Study of Christian Apocryphal Litera-ture (Association pour l'Étude de la Littérature Apocryphe Chrétienne; abbreviated AELAC) and on Oct 8 1982 an agreement was entered at Bruges between this Association and Brepols Publishers to publish in the *Corpus Christianorum* a *Series Apocryphorum*. The scholars behind the project are quite clear as to the reasons for this new series. They express it as follows[23]:

> Why this new series? The answer is simple: Christian apocryphal literature has come down to us in many languages. And there is no place for it in a series dedicated exclusively to Greek and Latin. A number of apocryphal texts have reached us not in their original language or only partially in that language but they have often left traces in versions preserved in a great variety of languages (Latin, Syriac, Coptic, Armenian, Georgian, Arabic, Slavonic, Old Irish). This new series aims at bringing together all these texts which contribute directly or indirectly to the knowl-edge of an apocryphal text. The advantage of presenting in *one* volume these different witnesses is twofold. The study of the texts is made easier and it can be seen how it has been transmitted and changed in different times and places.

Contact was established with the executive of AELAC in 1985 and sustained over the following years, with the result that in June 1988 an agreement was reached between the Irish Biblical Association, AELAC,

Corpus Christianorum and Brepols Publishers to have the Irish New Testament apocryphal literature critically edited, translated into English and published in the *Series Apocryphorum* in accord with the principles governing this Series. Thanks to the dedication of the Editorial Board of this new project (Professor Brian Ó Cuív, Dublin Institute for Advanced Studies,President; Dr Máire Herbert, Department of Early and Medieval Irish, University College, Cork and Professor Pádraig Ó Fiannachta, Department of Modern Irish, St Patrick's College, Maynooth), work has already begun on the material having to do with Apocryphal Infancy Narratives.

2.   Definition of Apocrypha

Any work treating of Apocrypha or Pseudepigrapha will of necessity have to come to terms with the question of definition, even if it fails to solve it satisfactorily. A collection of texts under one or other of these names will need to satisfy the editors and readers (not to speak of reviewers) as to why some items are included and others omitted. Both have also to deal to some extent with the question of the Canon of Scripture. By reason of the nature of the case a certain confusion will remain in this matter, as there was ambiguity in the ancient usage of the word apocrypha (which literally means "things that are hidden").

Traditionally the term has meant books, or sections of books, which were refused acceptance as part of the Canon of Scripture. Furthermore, with regard to the Old Testament there has been disagreement between Protestants and Catholics concerning these books and how to call them. In the traditional Protestant usage "Apocrypha" has been the name applied to the following fifteen books or portions of books: the First Book of Esdras, the Second Book of Esdras, Tobit, Judith, the Additions to the Book of Esther, the Wisdom of Solomon, Ecclesiasticus (or the Wisdom of Jesus the Son of Sirach), Baruch, the Letter of Jeremiah (in some editions incorporated as the final chapter of Baruch), the Prayer of Azariah and the Song of the Three Young Men, Susanna, Bel and the Dragon, the Prayer of Manasseh, the First Book of Maccabees, the Second Book of Maccabees. While not accepted as canonical these books have been held in regard by Protestants and were printed in a separate section, usually bound between the Old and New Testaments, but sometimes after the New Testament. Now, all these works, with the exceptions of the First Book of Esdras, the Second [also called Fourth] Book of Esdras and the Prayer of Manasseh are regarded as canonical by Catholics. Since their canonicity was agreed on later than that of the other Old Testament books they are called deuterocanonical. The Books of Esdras and the Prayer of Manasseh, Catholics regard and call apocryphal, agreeing in this with non-Catholic and general modern usage. The other non-canonical books relating to the Old Testament Catholics call Apocrypha, non-Catholics and general modern usage name them Pseudepigrapha. (It should be noted, however, that in the interests of uniformity, a number of Catholic scholars accept the general modern terminology with regard to the Apocrypha and Pseudepigrapha of the Old Testament.) The question is further complicated by the fact that some of the books designated in general as "Pseudepigrapha" are regarded as sacred and/or canonical by some Eastern Churches, e.g. the Book of Jubilees, the Book of Enoch (Ethiopic Enoch), Third and Fourth Maccabees. As a consequence, these two last-mentioned works are also included in some of the more recent "Common" English Bible translations.

With regard to the New Testament there is general agreement with regard to the Canon, which obviates the need of the dual designation "Pseudepigrapha" and "Apocrypha".

The problem with regard to the definition of "Pseudepigrapha" and "Apocrypha", however, does not end here. While there have been some lists of Apocrypha that were rejected, or described as not to be used inchurch, there is really no official list of what constitutes either group and editors have to choose and defend their choice[24]. The definition will probably depend somewhat on what a particular editor or group has in mind in the edition or study of the particular writings. The organisation AELAC, of which we have already spoken, has a broader definition than most, and one which takes account of later national developments from earlier Apocrypha. The admissibility of any particular writing must needs be discussed individually in accord with an overall definition accepted for a particular collection or project.

With regard to the Irish writings in which we are interested, a question will arise with regard to one or other of them as to whether they should be regarded in any real sense as Apocrypha. A case in question could be "The Evernew Tongue" which may be more in the nature of a medieval theological treatise than an apocryphal composition or the translation of an early one. This holds more so for the Irish texts known as "The Tidings of the Resurrection" and "Tidings of Doomsday".

Another factor complicating matters in this regard is the more or less ubiquitous presence of Jewish legends, midrash or haggadoth in early Christian writings, from which they passed over into medieval tradition. What is the dividing line between compositions using such traditions and apocryphal writings?

Together with the difficulties inherent in the nature of the Apocrypha themselves, many Irish writings apocryphal in character present a further problem in that they appear to be conscious imaginative compositions, amalgams of history, pseudo-history, the legendary and apocryphal. This holds in particular for compositions originating in Ireland in the tenth century and later. In his book *The Sources of the Early History of Ireland*, Professor James Kenney thus described this literature in 1929[25]:

> Chief among the classes of this later literature are:
> (6)... imaginative expositions of biblical and church history, of cosmic and eschatological ideas, based partly on the scriptures but mainly on Latin apocrypha and legends of continental origin. Although little of it has been preserved in its original form through Irish media, a vast amount of this Christian mythical lore must have been circulating in Ireland in the tenth, eleventh and twelfth centuries, some of it very curious and unusual and but little known elsewhere in Europe. It was all used freely and fully by what we may call popular writers in Irish on religious subjects. Indeed, all this later Irish ecclesiastical literature ... is characterised by an intense interest in the supernatural and the eschatological, and a constant delight in the wonderful and the bizarre.

Given this feature of Irish medieval literature and the inherent difficulty in defining Apocrypha, together with the fact that the study of the Irish material is still in its initial stages, it would appear unwise to apply too rigid an understanding of the term at the present moment. It may be possible to define more precisely as examination of the material progresses.

3. Transmission of Apocryphal Writings in Ireland

In our study of the knowledge and use of the Apocrypha in Ireland we must take of note of the nature of the evidence at our disposal, between direct and indirect transmission. We have direct transmission when we have actual texts of the Apocrypha as evidence. Sometimes, when this is lacking, we have to go on indirect transmission, through citations of the work in question — where this is available. Indirect transmission is something to be used with caution. Citations or echoes are not in themselves evidence for the presence of the entire apocryphal work. They might have come to a writer indirectly through some other work. However, such citations can be very illuminating, especially when there are a number of them, and can greatly add to the likelihood of the knowledge and use of an entire apocryphal work.

4. Historical Sketch of the Apocrypha in Ireland[26]

Writers on Latin ecclesiastical learning in early Ireland tend to divide the age into two periods: the foundational age, until A.D. 800, and another until the ending of the older order through the coming of the Normans, ca. A.D. 1200. Since the bulk of the Irish apocryphal writings are in Irish rather than in Latin, more natural divisions are (1) until A.D. 900; (2) from 900 until 1200; (3) the Norman period, A.D. 1200-1500.

i. *From the Beginning to A.D. 900.*

During this period religious education in Ireland seems to have been predominantly, although by no means exclusively, through the medium of Latin. Scholars who have studied the evidence are agreed that it was a period in which Apocrypha were widely used. In the words of Professor Bernhard Bischoff:

In the early period of Irish Christianity, one in many respects still dark, a refuge was offered for portion of the heretical and apocryphal literature which on the Continent was destined to disappear. The authentic form of Pelagius' commentary on the Pauline Epistles, and portion of the commentary on the Psalms by Theodore of Mopsuestia, were preserved there. Traces of the transmission of the *Gospel according to the Hebrews* and of other apocrypha also point to Ireland[26a].

David Dumville makes somewhat the same point towards the end of his study of the subject[27]:

We have, then, a confused picture of the position of the apocrypha in the eyes of the early Irish Church. What is perhaps clearest of all is that, beginning first with the semantic evidence—which pointed out the absence of a clear dividing line protecting the exclusivity of the Canon—and then considering the use of apocryphal works in liturgical and exegetical contexts, the early Irish seemed to have allowed themselves a remarkable freedom to use the apocrypha and appear generally to have held such works in a high regard which would have been impermissible elsewhere.

When we try to determine which Apocrypha were known and used during this early period, we possess only one full text, i.e. the Infancy Gospel of Thomas (in Irish), and this in a form which seems to indicate that it represents an Irish composition from traditional apocryphal material[28]. It has been argued that the apocryphon from which the Irish material on the death and assumption of Mary (the *Transitus Mariae*) derives must have been brought to Ireland in the seventh century[29]. The Irish texts in question, however, both Latin and Irish, are preserved in fifteenth century MSS, and the language of the Irish material is certainly later than the seventh century.

Source analysis of what appears to be Irish material from this period fills in the picture. From such an analysis of the apparently Hiberno-Latin text St Gallen Stiftsbibliothek MS 908 (MS 8-9 cent.) Charles D. Wright is able to deduce that the compilers of the florilegium had access to, and made use of, a wide range of apocryphal lore[30]. Wright notes specifically the use of 4 Esdras, the *Vita Adae et Evae*, the so-called

"Three Utterances" sermon (which dramatises the contrasting fate of a good and a bad soul as they are taken from their bodies at the moment of death), an account of the formation and naming of Adam deriving from eastern apocryphal sources but distinct from the Adam Octipartite apocryphon. There are points of contact, too, with the Questions of Bartholomew.

There is an abundance of apocryphal references in the Irish (Gaelic) Poems of Blathmac edited by Professor James Carney and assigned by him to ca. A.D.750[31]. The same holds true for a number of the other Latin and vernacular Irish writings from before A.D. 900 which still await publication or proper source analysis.

ii.   *From A.D. 900 to A.D. 1200.*

A new era in Irish learning began about A.D. 900. James Kenney has this to say about certain aspects of the literature of the new era:[32]

> The new age is distinguished not only by partially original works in Irish, but also by extensive translations from Latin into Irish. And the greater part of this literature, although falling into several different classes, has its own common and distinctive note.

One of these classes is the apocryphal literature and the imaginative expositions based mainly on Latin Apocrypha and legends of continental origin, as noted above in an earlier citation from Kenney's work. The bulk of the Irish texts of the Apocrypha date from this period, even though a number of them are preserved in manuscripts from a later date. From the earlier part of the period we have *Saltair na Rann* ("The Psalter of the Quatrains"), generally assumed to have been composed A.D. 988[33]. This work makes extensive use of two Apocrypha: for the opening part *The Book of Adam and Eve* (or *The Apocalypse of Moses*) and, for the final part, the *Apocalypse of Thomas*.

Among the Irish apocryphal compositions from around the tenth and eleventh centuries we have *Eve's Lament*, the *Evernew Tongue* (*Tenga Bithnua*) and *The Two Sorrows of the Kingdom of Heaven* (*Dá Brón Flatha Nime*). From the twelfth century we have the *Vision of Tundal*[34]. There are many others besides this, many of them preserved in manuscripts from the fifteenth century or later, and which, for this reason, we shall mention in the next section.

iii. From A.D. 1200 onwards.

There are indications that the Norman conquest in 1169 and later seriously affected Irish Latin ecclesiastical culture. One of the latest representatives of this seems to be *The Gospels of Máel Brigte* (MS. BL Harley 1802), written in the Armagh scriptorium in 1138. Although this branch of learning has not been fully researched, it does appear that the strictly Latin culture from the later period represents the newer Continental interests rather than the traditional and earlier Irish ones. Irish interest in apocryphal material, however, continued after the period of the Norman conquest, from 1169 onwards. Texts continued to be copied. In fact the largest collections of them are in manuscripts from the later period. Of these manuscript we need mention only two, the *Leabhar Breac* (Dublin, Royal Irish Academy 23 P 16),[35] and the *Liber Flavus Fergusiorum* (Dublin, Royal Irish Academy 23 O 48). The *Leabhar Breac* was compiled by one of the Mac Egans of Múscrige-Tíre, in northern Co. Tipperary, in or about A.D. 1411. It has the following items of apocryphal material: 1)The Passion of Stephen; 2)Revelation of the body of Stephen to the Presbyter Lucianus; 3)The Gospel of Nicodemus; 4)Passion of Peter and Paul; 5)Passion of Bartholomew; 6)Passion of Andrew; 7)Passion of Philip the Apostle; 8)Pedigrees and manner of death, etc. of the Apostles; 9)The manner of death etc. of the Prophets; 10)The Passion of Longinus; 11)Passion of John the Baptist. Together with this, there is the section (12) on the Teaching of the Maccabees and (13) a long tract on biblical history and pseudo-history as follows: a)on the creation and fall of Adam; b)on the history of the children of Israel, including a section on the covenant of the Lord with the children of Israel and another on the Ark of the Covenant. The New Testament section follows immediately on this with the following items: "On the Seventeen Wonders of the World on the Night Christ was born"; "On the Three Gospels read on the Night Christ was born"; "On the Shepherds of Bethlehem"; "On the Wise Men"; "On the Massacre of the Innocents"; "On the Flight into Egypt"; "On the Death of Herod"; "On the Death of Zacharias"; "On the Baptism of Christ", "On the Apostles"; "On the Household of Christ";

"On the Beginning of Christ's Preaching"; "On the Avenging of the Blood of Christ".

Scattered throughout the *Liber Flavus*, and without any particular order being apparent, we have the followingApocrypha or apocryphal pieces:The Fall of Lucifer and the Fall of Adam; The Penance of Adam; Distance of the Garden of Eden to the House of the Trinity; *Dá Brón Flatha Nime* ("The Two Sorrows of the Kingdom of Heaven"), apocryphal text on the Birth and Upbringing of Mary; Prose text on the Seventeen Wonders of the Night of Christ's Birth; Prose Version of the Letter of Jesus on Sunday Observance; Irish Translation of the Acts of Pilate; a Special text on the Harrowing of Hell; Dialogue of Our Lady and St Anselm on the Passion; Text on the Four Kinds of Wood from which Christ's Cross was made; the Finding of the True Cross; Irish Translation of the Passion of St Andrew; texts with Episodes from the Life of the Beloved Disciple (*Beatha Eoin Bruinne*); an Irish translation of the *Visio Sancti Pauli*; The Passion of Philip; Recension II of The Evernew Tongue; the *Transitus Mariae* (*Timna Muire*); Vision of the Two Deaths; Revelation of the Next Life made to a Priest; special text of the Fifteen Signs before Doomsday; the Seven Heavens.

The *Liber Flavus* was compiled in the fifteenth century. One feature of some of the apocryphal texts it carries is that the form of some of the apocryphal texts is demonstrably old. This is especially the case with regard to the *Transitus Mariae*[36] piece and also section of the *Beatha Eoin Bruinne*[37].

Apocrypha were also very much part of the Christianity, and of the new religious orders,that came with the Normans, even if these were of a somewhat different kind from the contemporary Irish ones. We do have some Apocrypha in Latin from this later period, all of them apparently representing new text forms brought in from abroad. We now know of four Latin texts from this period which were used in Ireland, even if not composed there, but there are probably more which have not yet been identified. These four are as follows:

1.   London, BL Royal 13.A.XIV (13th-14th cent.)[38]. A composite manuscript, written by nine different hands. It belonged at one time to the Dominican convent in Limerick, Ireland. Contains a variety of docu-

ments, including some Apocrypha: fol.195v-197r (by the fifth hand), a short Latin Gospel of Nicodemus[39]; fol. 260v-270v, the Gospel of Pseudo-Matthew, followed (270v) by a text on the Apostles and another (271-r-v) on the women of the New Testament; then 271v-272r:*In assumptione beatae Mariae...* Expl.*abierunt unusquisque ad patriam*. Ian Gijsel classes the Pseudo-Matthew text as Q[1]a3[40]. He believes that the Q family probably originated in the 11th century. The majority of the manuscripts representing it are either French or English.

2. Trinity College, Dublin 604; written in Britain ca. 1450[41]. It contains the following Apocrypha: fol. 55-63, the Gospel of Nicodemus; fol. 79-83 (by a different hand), Pseudo-Matthew. Gijsel classes this pseudo-Matthew text as Q[1]a4[42].

3. Trinity College, Dublin 312; 14th cent.,second part. A manuscript written in Britain in several Anglo-Saxon hands[43]. In fol. 127v-137v we have Pseudo-Matthew, which Gijsel classes as Q[2]a1[44].

4. Oxford, Rawlinson D 1236, 13th cent[45]. Apparently of English origin, this MS belonged to the Cistercian monastery of St Mary's, Dublin: Monasterium beatae Mariae Virginis iuxta Dublin. This MS contains only apocryphal material as follows: 1.fol. 1-22r, Vita Sanctae Mariae; 2. fol. 22r-37v, Pseudo-Matthew; 3. 37v-42v, Evangelium Thomae, without title; 4.a text, without title, connected with preceding: Inc. *Haec et alia plurima fecit Iesus praedicando et extollendo....*Expl. *...Et accepit omnes stupor de uerbo hoc et dicebant Benedictus qui uenit in nomine domini.*5.fol. 44v-49v, An Assumptio Mariae of Pseudo-Melito; 6. fol. 49r-60r, De aedificatione templi domini et origine ligni crucis domini nostri Iesu Christi; 6.fol. 60r-72r, Evangelium Nicodemi; 7.fol. 72r-74v, Vindicta Salvatoris. Gijsel classifies the text of Pseudo-Matthew as A[1]e4[46], a family represented by one French, one Swedish and two English MSS.

A Latin apocryphal writing that was brought into the island during this same period was *The Letter of Lentulus*, probably composed in the thirteenth century. It was translated into Irish in the sixteenth, and was apparently one of the latest texts to be translated into this vernacular[47].

5.   Extent of Irish Apocryphal Literature

In the work *The Apocrypha in the Irish Church*[48] the apocryphal material, or what might be suspected as Apocrypha, known in 1975 is listed under 108 distinct headings. Some of these headings have a number of subheadings, as for instance no. 91, "The Vision of St Paul (*Visio Pauli; Apocalypsis Pauli*)", with subdivisions 91A to 91F, and 104, "The Signs before Doomsday" with subdivisions 104A to 104J. While this brings the total number above 108, in another sense the higher figure is somewhat deceptive since some of the titles concern Apocrypha which may conceivably have been known in Ireland, but of whose presence there we have no clear evidence. Most of this Irish material has to do with the New Testament. The list of items dealing with the Old Testament is relatively limited.

From *Saltair na Rann* there is evidence for the presence in Ireland of the *Vita Adae et Evae* (the *Apocalypsis Mosis*). Other apocryphal material with Old Testament themes are compositions on the Creation and Fall, *De operibus Dei*, the Penance of Adam, Adam Octipartite, a Poem on Adam's head, the *Sex Aetates Mundi*. Based on the biblical evidence on Enoch and Elijah we have "The Two Sorrows of the Kingdom of Heaven"; there is legendary or apocryphal material connected with David and Solomon, which sometimes appears to be not much more than a garbled use of biblical evidence. We have Apocrypha using III and IV Esdras, and a piece on the Deaths of the Four Major Prophets. Together with this we have much material, some with apocryphal roots, on the sojourn of the Israelites in Egypt, on the Exodus and the connection of this with the ancestors of the Gaels.

We have a few Infancy Narratives[49], some of the Abgar material, the Letter of Lentulus on the personal appearance of Jesus, the Letter on Sunday observance, and texts on the Lord's Day. We have some of the generally known apocryphal material on John the Baptist, and texts combining this with Irish legends on the druid Mogh Ruith.

The traditional accounts on Harrowing of Hell are among the items, but also some other material on the same theme which appears to be more particular to Ireland[50].

The apocryphal material from Ireland on the Apostles is quite exten-sive[51]. The greater part of this represents the traditionally known *Acta Apostolorum Apocrypha*. A certain number of the items, however, are thus far known only from Irish sources, or from one or other rare text[52].

The Irish material on death and assumption of the Blessed Virgin Mary is limited in extent, but represents a very old form of the apocryphal *Transitus Mariae*[53].

We have a wealth of Irish apocryphal material on the Otherworld[54]. Some of it represents apocrypha known elsewhere. A certain amount of it, however, seems peculiarly Irish.

6.   The Importance of the Irish Apocrypha

All the apocryphal material of a country is of importance for one reason or another. It may bear witness to works generally known, and may be useful for evidence for particular recensions of these. It may contain evidence for early Apocrypha which elsewhere have either been lost or only partially attested. There is also the possibility that such Apocrypha may represent new national, and possibily vernacu-lar, creations from earlier apocryphal material. The Apocrypha known from Irish tradition are important from all these standpoints.

There are further reasons for the importance of the Irish Apocrypha. For instance, should we succeed in situating an individual Irish apocryphal item within the overall history of that given work, we may be able to determine the source, the area, from which it was first brought to Ireland, from where it ultimately derived and even the intermediaries in between. One scholarly position maintains that in Ireland we have very early Apocrypha of Eastern or even Syrian origin, which in the view of some came to Ireland through Visigothic Spain[55]. Future research will test the validity of such views. Then again, Irish apocrypha have been used as evidence of Irish influence on medieval continental European literature, particularly in the area of Visionary Literature and the Signs before Doomsday[56]. Here, as in the former case, only detailed study of the Irish material within the complete context of the Apocrypha will permit a solution to questions posed.

7.   Reason for the Present Choice

The texts selected for translation and publication in this volume have
been chosen for a variety of reasons. One guiding principle has been
the desire to present the reader with a representative selection of texts,
with regard both to the Old and the New Testaments, and within the
New Testament Apocrypha with regard to the various divisions -
Infancy Narrative, Public Life, Passion Narratives, Apocryphal Acts
of the Apostles, the *Transitus Mariae*, Visions of the Otherworld. Since
the Apocrypha traditionally known are readily available in English
translation, there seems no valid reason for including in a volume such
as this English translations of such Irish texts, when they differ little,
if at all, from that of the standard collections. However, in order to
have this type of Irish Apocrypha also represented, one or other of the
Irish texts of this kind are here included. Another major principle in
the presentation of the material is to translate here texts of which
translations have thus far not been published. In cases where both the
original and an English translation have been available, our aim has
been to translate from a manuscript text different from that previously
used.

This is the first such collection of Irish Apocrypha to be produced. The
Editors trust that it will give a good indication of the extent of this
branch of Irish literature and that it will serve scholars and the general
reader while we await the publication of the full corpus of Irish
Apocrypha. This we hope to see produced in the not too distant future.

8.   The Notes to the Texts

Given the present state of research in the field of Irish Apocrypha it has
been deemed best to present the translation without any elaborate
discussion of textual questions or of the issues involved. In the notes
at the end of the volume, for each text the manuscript indications are
given, often accompanied with a reference to M. McNamara, *The
Apocrypha in the Irish Church*, Dublin Institute for Advanced Studies,
1975, reprint 1984.

9.   A Note on the Translations
      By Máire Herbert

All of the translations in the present volume are my own. Some of the
texts had never before been translated. In other cases, I chose to
translate a hitherto unedited manuscript version of a particular text. I
have also made new translations of texts already rendered into English. Most of the existing translations date from the end of the last
century and the beginning of the present century. Only a few are
comparatively modern. In all cases, I have worked directly from the
manuscript texts, while taking account of existing published editions.
The texts vary in age from the eighth century to about the fourteenth.
We find both prose and verse, and a wide range of linguistic and
stylistic diversity. For the translator, therefore, each text presents its
own particular challenge. Previous translations of Irish biblical Apocrypha have reflected contemporary tastes, as well as editorial choice.
We find archaizing Biblically-modelled prose dominant in works of
the last century, while the demands of editorial accuracy have sometimes led to the publication by Celtic scholars of rather tortuous word
for word transference in place of translation.

I have sought to avoid these extremes of lavish paraphrase and over-
literalism, aiming at all times to produce an accurate and readable
rendering of the original. Yet, I am aware that, in seeking to negotiate
the distance between past and present, my own efforts must also be
tentative and subject to emendation. The Irish texts are distanced in
time from us, yet they themselves are also distanced from their own
sources. As we now mediate them to a new public, therefore, we look
forward to the revelation of fresh insights to enhance our understanding of their rich content.

Notes to Introduction

1   *The Old Testament Pseudepigrapha*, edited by James H. Charlesworth, vol.I. Apocalyptic Literature and Testaments; vol.II. Expansions of the "Old Testament" and Legends, Wisdom and Philosophical Literature, Prayers, Psalms, and Odes, Fragments of Lost Judeo-Hellenistic Works, London: Darton, Longman & Todd,1983, 1985; original U.S. edition by Doubleday Anchor Books. Also worthy of note is the same author's more recent review of research in the field: James H. Charlesworth, "Research on the New Testament Apocrypha and Pseudepigrapha", *Aufstieg und Niedergang der römischen Welt. Rise and Decline of the Roman World*, W. Haase and H. Temporini, ed., part II, Principate, vol. 25.5, Berlin-New York, 1988, pp. 3919-3968 ("Bibliography of Studies, Texts and Translations", 3940-3964).

2   Oxford: Clarendon Press; companion volume to M.R. James, *The Apocryphal New Testament*, Oxford:University Press,1924; reprint (corrected) 1953, 1955.

3   M.R. James, "Notes on Apocrypha", *JThS* 11(1909/10), 288-91; "Irish Apocrypha", *JThS* 20(1918/19), 9-16; *Latin Infancy Gospels. A New Text, with a Parallel Version from Irish*, edited with an Introduction by M.R. James, Cambridge:University Press, 1927.

4   "The Bringing forth of the Soul in Irish Literature", *JThS* 22(1920/21), 16-20; "Irish Versions of the *Transitus Mariae*", *JThS* 23(1921/22), 36-43; "Irish Versions of the Vision of St Paul", *JThS* 24(1922/23), 54-59; "The Seven Heavens in Irish Literature",*ZCP* 14(1923), 18-30; "The Eschatology of the Early Irish Church", *ZCP* 14(1923), 179-211; "The Book of Adam and Eve in Ireland", *PRIA* 36 C (1921-24), 121-33; "The Signs of Doomsday in the Saltair na Rann", *PRIA* 36 C (1921-24), 154-63; "Studies in the Vision of Tundal", PRIA 37 C (1924-27), 87-106; "Notes on Apocrypha in Ireland", *PRIA* 37 C (1924-27), 107-117; "The Vision of Adamnan", *PRIA* 37 C (1924-27), 304-312.

5   London: S.P.C.K., 1930.

6   *JThS* 23(1921/22), 36-43.

7   R. Willard, "The Testament of Mary. The Irish Account of the Death of the Virgin", *Recherches de théologie ancienne et médiévale* 9(1937), 341-64.

8   art. cit., 364.

9   ibid.

10   Charles Donahue, *The Testament of Mary. The Gaelic Version of the Dormitio Mariae together with an Irish Latin Version*, New York:Fordham University Press, 1942.

11   Victor Arras, *De Transitu Mariae. Apocrypha Aethiopice I* (Corpus Scriptorum Christianorum Orientalium. Vol. 343, Scriptores Aetiopici, tomus 67), Louvain: Secrétariat du Corpus SCO, 1973; see pp.vii-viii:"Magno in numero habendus est auctor qui in Irlanda *Testamentum Mariae* gaelice confecit. Quod ille solus narrationem retinuit de itinere in Aegyptum, quod solus probationem Pauli retulit et quod de itinere per transmundana testimonium servavit, satis est argumenti eius adhuc tempore codices graecos vel latinos exstitisse multo integriores codicibus nostris hodie notis. Hoc autem dolendum est quod qui acutiores de variis Transitibus scripserunt, hunc librum gaelicum, mole exiguum, momento vero magnum, utpote perrarum in europaeis vel maximis bibliothecis, inspicere non potuerunt. Qui expendere velit quomodo varii textus de Dormitione agentes, omnibus vestigiis indagatis, connexi sint, exoptabit fore

ut gaelicum scriptum rursus prelis subiciatur. Non enim sufficit legere quae optima de eo SEYMOUR et WILLARD exposuerunt; horum doctorum observationes ad unum tantum codicem, scil. Ms. 23048 b Dublinensis *Irisch*[!] *Academy* referuntur; cui nomen *Liber Flavus Fergusiorum* (XV saec.), quem SEYMOUR legit, DONAHUE vero suum textum sumpsit e codice *Laud. Misc. 610* Bibliothecae Oxoniensis (etiam XV saec.); codices alius ab alio discrepant, ut verbis DONAHUE suum apocryphum explanantis patet".

12   Michael van Esbroeck, "Les textes littéraires sur l'Assomption avant le Xe siècle", in *Les Actes Apocryphes des Apotres*, ed. F. Bovon, Genève:Labor et Fides, 1981,265-85, esp. 267, 271.

13   East Lansing: Michigan State College Press.

14   B. Bischoff, "Wendepunkte in der Geschichte der lateinischen Exegese im Frühmittelalter", in *Sacris Erudiri* 6(1954).189-279; in revised form in Dr Bischoff's collected essays: *Mittelalterliche Studien. Aufsätze zur Schriftkunde und Litteraturgeschichte*, Stuttgart:Hiersemann,1966, vol. I, 205-73. English translation by C. O'Grady, MSC in *Biblical Studies. The Medieval Irish Contribution* (Proceedings of the Irish Biblical Association no. 1), Dublin:Dominican Publications, 1976,73-160.

15   Bischoff, op. cit. (Eng. trans.),78,82.

16   James Carney, *Ériu* 18(1958), 1-43; id., *The Poems of Blathmac Son of Cú Brettan together with the Irish Gospel of Thomas and a Poem on the Virgin Mary* (Irish Texts Society, vol. 47), Dublin: Irish Texts Society, 1964, 89-105, 153-64.

16a   David Greene and Fergus Kelly, *The Irish Adam and Eve Story from Saltair na Rann*, volume I, Text and Translation   by David Greene and Fergus Kelly; volume II, Commentary by Brian O. Murdoch, Dublin Institute for Advanced Studies, 1976.

17   Fridericus Stegmüller, *Repertorium Biblicum Medii Aevi*, tom. I. Initia Biblica. Apocrypha. Prologi, Madrid:Consejo Superior de Investigaciones Científicas.Instituto Francisco Suárez, 1940.

18   *Repertorium Biblicum Medii Aevi*, vol. 8, Madrid, 1976; nos. 148, 15 (Letter of Jesus on SundayObservance), 164,24 (Transitus Mariae), 169,2 (Gospel of the Nazarenes), 176, 26 (Gospel of Thomas), 276,23 (Visio S. Pauli).

19   David Dumville, "Biblical Apocrypha and the Early Irish: A Preliminary Investigation", *PRIA* 73 C(1973), 299-338.

20   art. cit. 299 (In Abstract).

21   M. McNamara, *The Apocrypha in the Irish Church*, Dublin Institute for Advanced Studies, 1975 (reprint, with corrections, 1984). See reviews by Dáibhí Ó Cróinín in *Éigse* 16(part IV,1976), 348-56; David N. Dumville in *JThS* 27(1976), 491-94; H.-I. Marrou and P.-Y. Lambert in *Études Celtiques*   (1978), 738-39.

22   James H. Charlesworth (assisted by P. Dykers), *The Pseudepigrapha and Modern Research* (Society of Biblical Literature Septuagint and Cognate Studies, no. 7), Missoula, Montana;Scholars Press (for The Society of Biblical Literature), 1976, 26-27.

23   In the *Corpus Christianorum Series Apocryphorum* publicity pamphlet; also in François Bovon, "Vers une nouvelle édition de la littérature apocryphe chrétienne. La *Series apocryphorum du Corpus christianorum*", in *Gli Apocrifi cristiani e cristianizzati* (XI Incontro di studiosi dell'antichità cristiana), *Augustinianum* 23(1983),373-376

24   See the discussion on "Canonical and Apocryphal" and "The History of the New Testament Canon" by W. Schneemelcher in E. Hennecke, *New Testament Apocrypha*, edited by W. Schneemelcher; Eng. trans. by R. McL. Wilson, vol. 1, Gospels and Related Writings, London:Lutterworth Press, 1963, 22-64; J.H. Charlesworth, in *The Old Testa-*

ment Pseudepigrapha, vol. 1, xxiii-xxvii ("Canon, Definition of Pseudepigrapha, Writings Cognate with Pseudepigrapha"); earlier in *The Pseudepigrapha and Modern Research*, 17-25.

25   James F. Kenney, *The Sources for the Early History of Ireland: Ecclesiastical. An Introduction and Guide*, Columbia University Press, 1929 (later reprints, New York:Octagon Books, 1966; etc.), 733.

26   See M.McNamara, *The Apocrypha in the Irish Church* (note 21 above), 7-12.

26a   B. Bischoff, art. cit. (note 14 above), Eng. trans. 78; in *Sacris Erudiri* 195; *Mittelalterliche Studien* 210.

27   David Dumville, art. cit. (note 19 above),336. His position on the absence of due position for the Canon of Scripture in early Ireland could be queried.

28   See below, text no. 14, with notes.

29   See below, no. 24, with notes; also M.McNamara, *The Apocrypha in the Irish Church* (note 21 above), 122f.

30   Charles D. Wright, "Apocryphal Lore and Insular Tradition in St Gall, Stiftsbibliothek MS 908", in *Ireland and Christendom. The Bible and the Missions*, Proinséas Ní Chatháin and Michael Richter (eds.), Stuttgart:Klett-Cotta, 1987, 124-45, at 128.

31   For edition see James Carney, op. cit., note 16 above; for apocryphal references see D. Dumville, art. cit. (note 19 above), 305-312.

32   op. cit. (note 25 above), 732-33.

33   See M. McNamara, *The Apocrypha in the Irish Church* (note 21 above), 14-16.

34   See McNamara, op. cit., 11, 126f.

35   op. cit., 11f.

36   op. cit., 122f. and text no. 24 below, with notes.

37   op. cit., 95-98 and text no. 20 below, with notes.

38   On this MS see George H. Warner and Julius P. Gibson, *A Catalogue of Western Manuscripts in the Old Royal and Kings Library*, London, 1921, vol. II, 82-84; David J.G. Lewis, "A Short Latin Gospel of Nicodemus written in Ireland", *Peritia* 5(1986), 262-75 (at 262f.); Jan Gijsel, *Die unmittelbare Textüberlieferung des sog. Pseudo-Matthäus* (Verhandelingen van de koninklijke Akademie voor Wetenschappen, Letteren en Schone Kunsten van Belgie. Klasse der Letteren, Jaargang 43, nr 96), Brussels, 1981, 178-180. On J. Gijsel's book see Guy Philippart, "Le Pseudo-Matthieu au risque de la critique textuelle", *Scriptorium* 38(1984), 121-31.

39   edited by D.J.G. Lewis, art. cit., *Peritia*, note 38 above, 268-271.

40   Gijsel, op. cit., 178-180.

41   Thus Professor Martin L. Colker in the Catalogue of Medieval Latin Manuscripts in Trinity College, Dublin; see also Gijsel, op. cit., 180f.

42   Gijsel, loc. cit.

43   See Colker, op. cit. note 41 above; Gijsel, op. cit., 186f.

44   Gijsel. loc. cit.

45   See description in C. D. Macray, *Catalogi codicum manuscriptorum Bibliothecae Bodleianae*, part. V, fasc. 4, Oxford, 1898, cols. 371f.; Gijsel, op. cit.,55f.

46   Gijsel, loc. cit.

47   See McNamara, op. cit. (note 21 above), pp. 59f. (no.51A).

48   See note 21 above.

49   McNamara, op. cit., nos 35-50.

50   For Passion Narratives, see McNamara, op. cit., nos 58-69.

51   McNamara, op. cit., nos 72-96.
52   For instance episodes from the Life of John; cf. McNamara, op. cit., no. 83.
53   McNamara, op. cit., nos 97-98; below text no. 24, with notes.
54   McNamara, op. cit., nos 99-108.
55   See D. Dumville, art. cit. note 21 above.
56   Thus C. S. Boswell, *An Irish Precursor of Dante* (Grimm Library 18), London, 1908, for
       Fís Adomnáin, and for the Fifteen Signs before Doomsday, W.W. Heist in his work,*The
       Fifteen Signs before Doomsday*, East Lansing: Michigan State Press, 1952, following on St
       John D. Seymour (*PRIA* 36 C, 1923, 154-160).

TEXTS

translated by

Máire Herbert

THE OLD TESTAMENT

1.THE CREATION OF ADAM

1 Adam was created in the third hour, for seven hours he was without sin, and on the tenth hour he was expelled from Paradise.

2 These are the seven components from which Adam was made. The first was of earth, the second of sea, the third of sun. The fourth was from clouds, the fifth, wind, the sixth, stones. The seventh was the light of the world.

3 Let us continue concerning these matters. The first part, formed of earth, was his trunk. The second part, of sea, was his blood. The third part, formed from the sun, was his countenance and face. The fourth part, from the clouds, consisted of his thoughts. The fifth part, from wind, was his breath. The sixth part, formed from stones, constituted his bones. The seventh part, from the light of the world, namely. the Holy Spirit, was the man's soul.

4 If, in the case of any person, the earthen part predominates, that person will be slothful. If it be the sun, he will be fair and lively. If it be the clouds, he will be light-weight and lustful. If the wind predominates, he will be fiery and angry. If it be the stones, he will be harsh, and he will be both a thief and a covetous person. If it be the sea, he will be lovable and docile, and he will have beauty. If the predominant part is the light, he will be single-minded, and will be filled with the grace of the Holy Spirit and divine scripture.

2.CREATION AND FALL

1 There were nine orders and nine grades among the angels. The Lord said to Lucifer: "All the hosts of archangels will be subject to you. Now let you render homage to Adam, my own likeness". Lucifer said: "I will not render homage to Adam, for I am senior to him, and more noble, and I will not bow down before my junior". The Lord said to him: "You will not be honoured by me if you do not submit to Adam". Lucifer replied with arrogance and pride: "I will be king over all the hosts of angels, and they will serve me. I will establish my dwelling in the north-east of heaven in a remote place, and there will be no other king over me". Thereupon Lucifer, with all his host, was cast down from heaven on account of his pride, and he was driven into eternal hell. Now some writings say that a thousand years elapsed between the creation of the angel until his transgression. Other records say, however, that thirteen and a half hours was the length of time from the creation of the angel until he transgressed.

2 The King made a pleasant abode for man in the beginning, that is, Paradise, a fruitful land of many melodies. He arranged a well with four streams, one stream each of wine, oil, new milk, and honey, as sustenance for the blessed creatures. And he gave each of these streams in turn a name, so that we have Phison, Gehon, Tigris, and Euphrates. Phison, the stream of oil, flowed eastward. Tigris, the wine, flowed westward. Euphrates, the honey, flowed southward. Gehon, the milk, flowed northward. Moreover, a wall of red gold surrounded Paradise.

3 Then Adam was created. After his creation he remained for three days without a soul, thus prefiguring the resurrection of Christ. A name was then assigned to him, formed from the four stars, which were named, respectively, Anatole, the eastern star, Dusis, the western, Archon, the northern star, and Missimbria, the southern. These are the names of the four sods out of which Adam was created: Malon, Arton, Biblon, and Agore. From Malon his head was formed, from Arton, his chest, from Biblon, his belly, and from Agore, his feet. The first sight

which Adam saw after he had received a soul was the mountains of Pariath.

4   From the eighth upper rib of the chest on Adam's right side Eve was formed to be his equal...Now, the reason why Adam's body was formed from the common earth was that it was known that it would be defiled. Thus it was from the pure, unpolluted earth of Paradise that the body of Mary was formed subsequently, since it was from the body of Mary that Christ's body was to be born, according to the truth of holy scripture, as well as the prophets and patriarchs. This is the name of the place where Adam was created, *in agro Damasgo*. He proceeded from there to Paradise.

5   Nine months passed from the time that Adam received a soul until Eve was fashioned from his side. And this is the precedent for the manner in which every woman of their seed thereafter carries a child. Then the Lord announced to Adam and Eve together: "You may eat all the fruits of Paradise, save for that of one tree alone, so that you may know that you are under my rule and power. You will suffer neither decline nor illness, and you will be borne bodily to heaven at the age of thirty". Lucifer was jealous of Adam, being certain that it was Adam who would be brought to heaven in place of himself.

6   God granted that all the animals who possessed body and life should be subject to Adam. Thus it was the latter who exercised power over then. While the hosts of the seven heavens came to the High-king, every animal in the world came to Adam, to do him honour and worship, and to delight him. It was the Lord, indeed, who directed them to place themselves in front of Paradise, in sight of Adam. Each then returned to its abode, after saluting Adam.

7   The devil, however, was casting about for a way to deceive Adam. The resolve on which Lucifer settled was that he should go to the outside of Paradise in the midst of the animals. There he found the serpent at the extremity of the whole group. "It is not at all just", said the devil to the serpent, "that you should be thus on the outside, despite your cleverness and cunning. For it is a great wrong that the most junior being in creation should be honoured above you. It would not be a major crime to cause harm or temptation to befall him, since you were

created before Adam, and you should not have to bow to your junior".

8   Then the devil said to the serpent: "Take my advice", said he, "and let us make a pact and an alliance. Do not go to Adam. Rather, allow me to enter your body, and let us both go to Eve to prevail on her to eat the fruit of the prohibited tree, in order that she may induce Adam thereafter to do the same. Thus they will transgress the command of their lord, and will lose the favour of God thereby, and they will then be expelled out of Paradise". The serpent asked: "What is my payment for this, that I should allow you to cohabit in my body for the purpose of ruining Adam and Eve?" "You shall have as a reward", said the devil, "that the two of us are named together forever after".

9   Then Lucifer assumed the form of the serpent, and went to the gate of Paradise. The serpent called from outside, saying: "O Eve, wife of Adam, speak with me". "I have no time to talk to anyone", said Eve, "for I am looking after all the brute animals". "If you be Eve, it is you whom I urge to act in my interests", said the serpent. "When Adam is not here, it is I who am guardian of Paradise, and I look after all the animals", said she. "Where does Adam go from you when he is not present to see to the animals?", asked the serpent. "He goes to adore the Creator", said Eve.

10   "Tell me, Eve, is your life in Paradise agreeable?", asked the serpent. "There is nothing greater sought by us than to be in Paradise until we go bodily to heaven", said Eve. "For every good created by God in Paradise is at our disposal, except for one tree alone. We were commanded not to eat any of the fruit of that tree, and we were told that if we ate it we would die".

11   The serpent said to Eve: "Neither your knowledge nor your wisdom is any greater than that of every brute animal. Your lord did not give you knowledge of evil, only of good alone. This is a great deficiency in you, and you are being deceived by not being allowed to eat any of the fruit of the tree in which is the knowledge of good and evil". The serpent continued: "This is why that tree was devised, and why you are not allowed to eat from it, so that you should not have the ability to know both good and evil. Do not be slow. Go to the tree to taste of it, and if you eat but one apple from the tree, you shall have knowledge

of good and evil from your lord himself".

12 Eve said to the serpent: "Though your counsel and plan is fine, I do not dare go to the tree lest I die". She added: "Go yourself, serpent, to the tree, and bring the apple to me, so that I may divide it with Adam, in order to discover whether what is promised of it be true". Then the serpent said to Eve: "Open the gate of Paradise to me, so that I may bring you the apple from the tree". "If I open the gate of Paradise, and if you go in, do not delay there except to bring me the apple from the tree", said Eve. The serpent replied to Eve: "Provided that I get from the tree the apple which will enable you to distinguish between evil and good, I will go out afterwards, lest I be confined or made captive".

13 Then Eve opened the gate for the serpent, and he went rapidly towards the prohibited tree. He picked the apple, and gave it to Eve. She ate half, and left the other half for Adam. Suddenly, after Eve had eaten the apple, her form and appearance changed. The gleaming garment which was around her fell off, shivering and cold seized her, and she was astonished to find herself naked. Thereupon she let out a terrible cry to Adam. The latter came at Eve's call, and was amazed to find her naked. Adam said to Eve: "You will not survive as you are, without your clothing. What has befallen you?" "I will not tell you ", said Eve, "until you eat the half of this apple which is in my hand". Adam took the half of the apple, and ate it. And his garments fell off, so that he was stark naked, like Eve.

14 Then Adam said: "O Eve, who has deceived you, and deceived me along with you? It is that Lucifer", said he, "and so we will be henceforth and forever subject to hardships and numerous diseases". Eve replied: "It was the serpent who asked me to let him into Paradise, and after he entered he got me an apple from the prohibited tree, and said : 'O Eve, take this apple from me, so that you may be able to distinguish both good and evil. Divide it between you and Adam', said he. I took the apple then, and I was aware of no harm resulting from it until I saw myself naked. I knew no evil before then. It is that serpent who has ruined us, O Adam", said Eve.

15 Adam then said to Eve: "Would that you had not happened upon your apple. It is evident to us that we are destined to endure much evil

henceforth, now that we are naked. Moreover, there is something even worse in store for us, the separation of body from soul, the decay of the body in the earth, and the consignment of the soul to eternal hell". As all their clothing had fallen from them, thereafter they were filled with depression and misery, and they felt it shameful that their bodies had no protecting veil over them. Thus each of them saw clearly the colour of each other's body, so they then took fig leaves to cover their nakedness. There was not found in Paradise any tree bearing foliage save the fig-tree only.

16   Then Adam heard the voice of Michael the archangel, saying to the angel Gabriel: "Let the horn and summoning trumpet be sounded, so that they may be heard throughout the seven heavens, and let all of you go to meet your creator". And all hosts and throngs of angels of the seven heavens arose, and proceeded together to Paradise to their maker. Then the Lord came to them with his great host to Paradise, surrounded by choirs of angels singing. Cherubim sat by the royal seat of the High-king in Paradise, in the very centre of Paradise, moreover, where the tree of life was situated. A pleasant site, indeed, was Paradise. Each host was drawn up according to rank, and each grade was surrounded by its angels. The King himself sat in his royal seat above Cherubim. Then the trees and woods of Paradise bowed down to the ground to show honour to the Creator.

17   Thereupon God said to the company of heaven: "Have you heard of the deed done by Adam, which insulted me, and transgressed my precept and teaching?" At that, Adam and Eve took shelter under the tree, in flight from the voice of the Creator. Then Adam made this harmful utterance: "If I have violated your command, it was the woman whom you bestowed on me, namely Eve, who tempted me". God replied to Adam: "Since you do not acknowledge your guilt, your family will be forever contending against you. If you had shown repentance, what you did would be forgiven you, and you would be in your primeval state of prosperity".

18   God then gave this order to his angels: "Send Adam out of Paradise and to the common earth again". Thereafter, angels expelled Eve and Adam out of Paradise. And then there came upon them sorrow and dejection, poverty and hunger, anger and grief, and numerous differ-

ent diseases. Thereupon Adam said to the angels of heaven: "Grant me a little delay, so that I may taste some of the fruit of the tree of life". "You will not taste any of that tree of life for as long as your body and soul are joined together", they said. And then, indeed, Adam was parted from Paradise from that time henceforth.

3.THE PENANCE OF ADAM

1   God granted this common earth to Adam and Eve after their transgression in Paradise. After expulsion from Paradise Adam remained for a week without drink or food, without clothing or shelter or fire, overcome by remorse and grief. And they were reproaching and mutually blaming each other. Adam said: "Great was the bounty bestowed on us, if only the devil had not tempted us to defy the Lord. We could converse with angels, and all of God's creatures honoured us. Fire could not burn us, nor water drown us, weapon-blade could not lacerate us, nor could disease overcome us. Now, every element is in opposition to us, for sake of the honour of the Lord. It is not God who is to be blamed, but we ourselves".

2   Eve said to Adam: "The guilt is mine", said she."Put me to death, O Adam, since it is more likely that God would show mercy to you". "We have offended the Lord sufficiently already ", said Adam. "I will not slay you, my kin", said he, "for you are miserable and naked even now, and I will not spill my own blood on the ground, since you are part of my own body. It is not right to perpetrate another offence against the Lord lest he destroy us, lest he hand us over to demons in the depths of hell, and consign us to the domains of Lucifer. For we are already in extreme pain, and we may die of cold and hunger, since we have been for twelve hours without food or clothing". Then Eve said: "Why do you not journey in every direction, man, to see if you can find something for us to eat?" Adam rose and traversed around in search of food which they could consume, but he found only the herbs of the earth, the food of the brute animals. After the foods of Paradise they found this sustenance disagreeable.

3   Then Adam said to Eve: "Let us repent and do penance, and put away from us some of our sins and transgressions". Eve said: " Instruct me, for I do not know how to do penance". Adam replied: " Let us adore the Lord, and keep silence, with neither of us speaking to the other. Let you go to the river Tiber, and I will go to the river Jordan", said he. "Let you remain for thirty-three days in the Tiber, and I shall be for forty-

seven days in the Jordan. Take with you a stone slab to put under your feet, and let the water come up to your neck, and let your hair spread loose on either side of you on the surface of the river. Raise your hand towards the Lord, direct your gaze towards the heavens and beseech the Lord to forgive you for your offence".

4   Eve said:" I am too defiled to pray to God, since my flesh is corrupted". Adam replied to Eve:" Let us implore all of creation brought into being by pure prayer, so that all may beseech the Lord with us for forgiveness of our transgression. Let us fulfill the task, and let us not be distracted".

5   Adam remained for forty-seven days thereafter in the river Jordan, while Eve was thirty-three days in the river Tiber. And angels came from God every day to speak to Adam and to instruct him for a period of nineteen days. Then Adam implored the river Jordan with its many creatures to fast with him to God for forgiveness of his offence. Then the river stood still, as did every living creature in it. They assembled about Adam , and they all prayed, the animals and the river included. They directed a great lament toward all the heavenly orders who are around the Lord that Adam might be forgiven for his offence against God, and be granted complete pardon of his sin. They asked for a habitation on earth, and, after the separation of soul from body, a heavenly dwelling for Adam himself, and for his family and descendants after him, save for whoever disregarded the precept of the Lord.

6   The devil heard this utterance, and in the guise of an angel of God he went again to Eve in order to lure her out of the river and impede her penance. He said to her: "You have been a long time in the river Tiber, O Eve, and though your appearance used to be pleasing, there has been a change in your looks and form. You have destroyed and ruined yourself. Come quickly out of the river. God sent me to take care of you, and to take you from the river". Eve then came out of the water and as she was drying herself on the bank she was overcome by a faint which left her nearly lifeless.

7   Thus Eve did not recognize that it was Lucifer who had assumed the appearance of an angel of God, and her mind was perplexed. Lucifer said to Eve: "You are deliberating greatly, O Eve. It is by order of God

in heaven that I have come to you. Let us go from here to Adam", said he, "so that we may beseech the heavenly God to grant you both forgiveness of your sins". They went then to the place where Adam was, in the river Jordan. When Adam saw Eve and Lucifer he was seized by trembling and loathing at the appearance of the devil. "Alas, Eve", said Adam, "you have been deceived by the one who deceived you already in Paradise. I am grieved that you left the river Tiber before an angel of God had come to bring you out".

8   When Eve heard Adam's rebuke she collapsed on the ground, and came close to sudden death. Then Adam said:" O Lucifer, devil, why are you pursuing me? You caused our banishment from Paradise and took pleasure in our expulsion. You have brought me to dejection. But your relegation to hell was not caused by us, but by trespass against the King of Heaven. It was not us who urged you to act with pride and disobedience against the Lord".

9   Lucifer said to Adam: "All the misfortune which I have suffered came upon me because of you, and I will tell you how it happened. We were both put out of heaven. When your soul was joined to your body and you were created in the likeness of God, all were asked to do you reverence. Michael was sent to you from heaven and he brought you to adore the creator. When you had adored the King of the heavenly planets, he ordered all of creation to honour you eternally. Then God sent Michael throughout the seven heavens to get angels and archangels to come in their hosts to pay homage to his likeness. And Michael told me that I would be foremost of all.

10   Thereafter I came and seated myself before the Lord. And the King said to the nine grades of angels and to the host of heaven: "Let you do honour and reverence to my likeness, Adam". Then Michael said:" It is fitting for every heavenly order to pay homage and respect to your likeness". Thereupon I said that Adam was not the most senior of all creation, and that it was not proper that the senior should do honour do the junior. Then a third of the heavenly host, both angels and archangels, said that my statement was justifiable. The King then said to his company:" It is the junior who is to be regarded as the highest in heaven for as long as I dwell there". I said that I would not go to pay homage to Adam even if all others did so, because I was the most

senior. Thereafter I was immediately cast out of heaven on your account, O Adam, since I opposed the will of God. All of our host, a third of the household of heaven, were sent to hell, while you remained in Paradise after us. You would have had a fortunate life afterwards, if no change had come upon you".

11 "I say to you, O Adam", said Lucifer, "that every harm and trouble which you will suffer will be caused by me, and all my evil-doing will be directed at you, O Adam. Moreover, I will bring your family and descendants into conflict and strife, misfortunes and pestilences, diseases and great tribulations for as long as they live, because of my hostility to you".

12 Then Adam came out of the river after completing forty-seven days of penance, and Lucifer departed. Adam and Eve remained in a state of depression and shame afterwards. For a year the couple were alone, with no sustenance except the herbs and grass of the earth to eat, like every brute animal, and water drunk from the palms of their hands. They had neither clothing or shelter or fire, remaining under the shade of trees or in the dry caves of the earth.

4.THE DEATH OF ADAM

1 Let you know without doubt Adam's life-span. It was not short. He had truly nine hundred and thirty years of life.

2 Then a thorough illness came on Adam, as it comes on all. His wife, Eve, in every way excellent, awaited his final testament.

3 Adam knew his condition, and said to fair and modest Eve: "I am going to die from this illness, and be parted from you, and from your offspring".

4 "A pity before God that you should not be remaining here, and that it is not I who is going first", said Eve clearly to Adam.

5 "Alas for your deterioration, O Adam", said Eve. "I shall be wretched and without strength here, since you are going first".

6 "O excellent and comely Eve, understand clearly that it is evident that you will not be here in torment for long after me".

7 "Truly, there was a short span of time between our creations. Thus it is clear that you will be only nine months in suffering after me".

8 "Tell me without shortcoming, O husband, what I shall do with your beloved body, since you are sure that your death is at hand, O my lord Adam".

9 "Let neither foot nor hand touch me. Let nobody come to disturb me, until there shall be a message from God in heaven concerning the disposition of my dear body".

10 "Do not move my corpse from its confinement - an agreeable task. I am assured that the noble creator who fashioned me will provide for my body".

11 "Rise up diligently, Eve, and keep a cross-vigil. Let you utter a fitting call to God that my soul goes clearly to heaven".

12   "The soul which God has created for me, he has summoned, though it be unclean. Let it come to him intact, to his dwelling in the company of the angelic host".

13   "O wife, as regards my good King, may he not bestow on me truly the anger which he [formerly] showed - a clear course. May we have tenderness and mercy".

14   "O Eve, beseech the glorious King that he may come in excellence to meet me, and if he does not come at my impetuous endeavour, may the archangel Michael come".

15   Eve rose and turned towards the ground, weeping and lamenting greatly. For the space of an hour she was engaged thus, wretchedly and tearfully.

16   "I beseech you, O my King", said fair Eve, "is it fitting for us to speak in your presence, since we have adored you here?"

17   "My transgression and offence is so great that, unless I remain in constant penitence, and unless you grant me forgiveness, I am not able to speak with purity".

18   The wretched Eve knelt down on the ground, and said resolutely: "O King of heaven, I direct my tears to you until the warrior Michael comes to me, to cleanse the soul of Adam, to relieve him of his faults, and to guide him after death to the hosts of archangels".

19   "Rise up from the ground, O Eve. Your words have assuredly been heard. Your tidings have reached the pinnacle of heaven. The warrior Michael has come to you".

20   "O fair Eve, Adam's soul has departed from his body. With your two hands arrange with affection his fair countenance, a good and precious task".

21   Thereafter, Eve hastened to beloved Adam, and found that he was not breathing.

22   When the fair Eve did not hear the voice of Adam reply to her, this overcame her mind, and brought on immoderately excessive weeping and continuous sorrowing.

23   "O Eve, look up, and allow me to instruct you. Direct your keen pure gaze assiduously upwards to the heavens".

24   "O woman, lift up your fair countenance, and see the soul of Adam as it is borne resplendently in the midst of hosts of archangels".

25   Then Eve turned to look at the soul of Adam, and she saw his beloved gentle soul accompanying Michael.

26   As Eve then was recognizing the soul of Adam, she saw a host of choir-singing angels approach it on its journey.

27   After that, Eve saw the seraphim with noble movement in front of the host. Beautiful was the beloved one whom it raised up with three golden wings.

28   Thereafter, Eve saw across the sky three bright resplendent birds. She was dumb-struck by their brilliance.

29   As she looked eagerly at the birds, they appeared so like rays of bright sun that she could not gaze at them.

30   The choir of holy angels surrounding Michael was heard as far as misty heaven. The ranks arrayed themselves nobly and distinctively around Adam at the altar.

31   The angels surrounding the altar sang fitting harmonies. In front of every host they burned the herb called ornamentum.

32   The strong smoke was directed straight up through the atmosphere, so that it opened wide the gates of the firmament.

33   And God came in holiness from heaven to receive the soul of Adam. The royal Prince, the ruler over every place, sat on his throne.

34 One splendid angel from among the angelic host went, with pure course, before the great King, and pleasantly played clear pure music. Its beautiful sound extended throughout the seven heavens.

35 At the sound of the trumpet, the entire host of the nine [angelic] orders came in splendour. Their bright company was truly impressive in front of the royal seat of the Creator.

36 They sang together, a most beautiful thing, in companies and in choirs: "Blessed at all times is the High King of every essence".

37 All the complete host of the pure holy angels bowed down to the ground. They beseeched [their] beloved God to forgive the offence of Adam.

38 "O King, who created your likeness out of nothing, we implore you, in your love, have mercy on him".

39 Thereupon the mighty king sent the seraphim, with wings of red gold, swiftly along the slopes by the side of the host.

40 It took the soul of Adam without difficulty, and bathed it in the stream of ...

41 Then it took the bright pure soul of Adam out of that stream, and placed it foremost before the countenance of the Creator.

42 The soul of Adam, with fair love, threw itself on the ground, and remained lying before the mighty King for the space of three full hours.

43 Then the King placed his hand over the head of the soul of Adam, and commended him unstintingly to Michael - pleasant to report.

44 "O Michael, do not be remiss in taking great care of the soul of Adam, which has placed itself here in Paradise".

45 "Take with the hosts the bright pure soul of noble Adam, and place it in the peaceful gathering in the third royal section of Paradise".

46   God said: *"In tertio caelo*, which is called Ficconicia, there let him be,
      without sign of pain, until the time of the resurrection".

47   Melodious was the clear choral-singing of all the orders of every place,
      both angels and archangels, as they praised the Creator for remitting
      his sins and faults from Adam's soul, and for bringing him back to
      Paradise without hostility.

48   "Let you yourselves put the oil of mercy and the herb ornamentum
      around the body of Adam to cleanse it of its faults".

49   "Let three perfect linen cloths be arranged around the body of Adam
      - a noble deed. Then let it be buried carefully beside the grave of Abel".

50   Then, according to many learned sources, there was buried long ago in
      Hebron the body of our forefather Adam, in the sorrowful harsh
      captivity of death.

51   The body of Adam remained honourably in its burial-place until it met
      with the fierce wave of the deluge, in harsh circumstances.

52   The waves of the deluge over every plain, which razed many lands,
      took away Adam's head, and brought it to Jerusalem.

53   Thereafter, the head remained at the gate of Jerusalem. Later, the cross
      of Christ was fixed without misfortune in the body of Adam.

5.ADAM AND HIS DESCENDANTS

1 The face of Adam, of noble appearance, looking eastward at the Mount of Partech in Paradise, was gladdened at the sight of the sun over the summit of the great mountain.

2 "Let us adore, let us adore you, O God", was the first cry he uttered. When he saw the beauty of Eve, he smiled for the first time.

3 His first walk, an unhindered celebration, was to the well of Partiach in Paradise. He first ran, with swift step, in order to see the birds.

4 For fifteen days, - this is no deception - Adam and Eve were together, until there came to them a demon [fallen] from heaven, to tempt them on a Friday.

5 The demon, with evil intent, assumed the form of the serpent, a very opportune body. The letters which he used for a grevious chant were Iae, Uau, Ia, Iath.

6 Here is the known reason why "left" has connotations beyond those of "right". It results from the fact that it was the crooked left hand which was reached out to the apple.

7 After their unlawful transgression, they were cast into the lofty land of Egypt. For a period of three months after the rout, a single palm-tree provided food and shelter for them.

8 Cain was conceived - I do not conceal it - as also was Abel. The action of the curse adhered to Cain, the decrepit creature of bondage.

9 Abel and Cain, without concealment, went to sacrifice two rams. The glorious King did not accept the sacrifice which Cain had brought.

10 The powerful grace of the King descended on the sacrifice of Abel. As a result, Cain, the sinful and treacherous man, was filled with envy and anger.

11   In his violent hand Cain seized the blameworthy jaw-bone of a camel.
     He leapt furiously on Abel, and killed him with a single blow.

12   We are told by the experts, those men of melodious learning, that from
     ancient times the stones did not grow, once the blood of Abel had
     touched them.

13   Thereafter, seven swellings came on the body of Cain as a result of his
     kin-slaying. There was a lump on each of his two feet, and two lumps
     for his hands.

14   There was a protuberance on his forehead, alas, and one on each of his
     two cheeks. It was the grievous lump on his forehead that was struck
     by the cast of Lamiach.

15   The forceful Lamiach, the bigamist, was the first man to take two
     wives. By his hand dishonourable Cain fell, after Lamiach had thrown
     the apple at him.

6.THE TWO SORROWS OF THE KINGDOM OF HEAVEN

1 Why is there mention of sorrow in heaven? The solution is not difficult. Elijah and Enoch implored the Lord that they should be conveyed bodily to heaven. So, because of their outstanding merit in the service of God on earth, they were borne to Paradise in their human form. There, round about them in flight, were the bright, clear, weightless souls, light as air, in the form of angels. But Elijah and Enoch were in their earthly, heavy, inert bodies, and were not able to be alongside them. They were greatly saddened and grieved not to be in the company of the angels. Thus we have the two sorrows of the kingdom of heaven.

2 Elijah went as far as the tree of life in Paradise, to preach, with gospel-book in hand, to the birds there. The birds came, and were eating the berries of the tree. These were large berries, sweeter than all honey, and more intoxicating than every wine. They continued eating the berries. Then Elijah opened the gospel. With that, the birds pressed their wings and feet to their bodies, and stirred neither wing nor foot until the sermon ended.

3 He preached to them about the Day of Judgement, in particular, about the tortures to be meted out to the souls of certain persons on Doomsday. The four rivers around Mount Sion would be assigned to burn souls for ten thousand years (and there are ten hundred years in each thousand). Thus, a great amount of distress awaits the sinner. Fortunate is he who has accumulated goodly merit, even on that day itself. For though a person had no other anxiety but judgement-day, yet, as long as he lives, he should not rest from thinking about it. Moreover, he should contemplate the coming of Christ, with the nine grades of heaven, with all earthly men ever born, and ever to be born, and with the host of hell. Thus will Jesus Christ appear with his reddened cross on his back, to avenge his crucifixion on them as he comes to save them from the maw of the devil.

19

4   The host assembled there will be enormous. Moreover, it is in the
     presence of that host that all will set forth their deeds, both good and
     bad. Each in turn when requested will reveal what his eyes saw, what
     his mouth and tongue said, what was done by his hands, and what was
     traversed by his feet. Christ, son of God, along with the angels of
     heaven, and the inhabitants of earth and of hell, will be listening to all
     until the revelations are completed. Each person will be reminded of
     every wrong which he committed by his accompanying demon, who
     keeps watch on him constantly at his left side. On his right, moreover,
     is his attendant angel who will recall for him all the good which he has
     done.

5   After all of this is completed, Christ declares: "Consider, O judges,
     whether the good done by this man outweighs the evil". When the
     good triumphs Christ says: "Enter, then, into the company of angels".
     The angels come to meet him with arms outstretched. "Welcome", say
     all. [In another instance, one hears]:" He will come to me. That man has
     good and evil in equal measure. Half of him belongs to me", says the
     devil. "The soul will not be divided", says Christ, " and since my
     power is the mightier, he will go with me". In the case of the man in
     whom evil predominates, [he is told] to go in his wickedness to those
     whom he has chosen. Demons come to meet him, and treat him with
     hostility. At last, when the decisions about the fate of the children of
     Adam are completed, then Christ will bid those who have chosen thus
     to depart with the devil and his rabble, to be cast into his company in
     the eternal abyss. These will rise then, uttering a single cry as the devil
     drags them with him to hell.

6   There are, indeed, three particular cries in the world. There is the cry
     made by the people of God as they were being forced by Pharaoh and
     the Egyptians towards the Red Sea, to be slain and exterminated, and
     their sons and daughters enslaved forever, unless God delivered
     them. Then there is the cry of the inhabitants of hell, and the souls of
     those of the children of Adam who died before the crucifixion of
     Christ, that is, those whom he took to spite the devil, so that they came
     to the abodes of the kingdom of heaven. The cry, therefore, is that
     uttered by the souls in their delight at escaping from the devil, and the
     cry of the denizens of hell left behind. The third cry is that of the souls
     of those who merit hell, as they are being dragged off to the eternal

dwelling of pain and torture, which has no end. Those, however, chosen by God, will go to the eternal kingdom with Christ, son of God, to remain there forever among the hosts of archangels.

7   Thus Elijah preaches of the distress of Doomsday, as we have mentioned already, though we relate here only a few things out of many. Then when the cleric closes his book, the birds emit a cry, and beat their wings against their sides until streams of blood flow from them, in terror before the Day of Judgement.

8   Now this Elijah and Enoch, of whom we have been speaking, await their slaying and martyrdom in fulfillment of the prophecy of the Lord, uttered through the mouth of the prophet: *Quis est homo qui uiuit et non uidebit mortem*? "Who has tasted of life who will not taste death?" At the end of the world they will oppose Antichrist, who will be put to the sword by them. A demon in human form is this Antichrist, in the guise of one who comes to spread faith. A bishop will beget him on his daughter on a Friday. It is said that there is no miracle performed by Christ on earth that he will not perform, except for the raising of the dead. However, he will be full of lust and falsehood. He will be thirty-three and a half years old, the same age as that of Christ. The inversion of his writing-tablet in front of him is a sign by which he will be recognized. He will put to the sword everyone who does not believe in him, for he will declare himself to be the son of God, one who was foretold by prophets. It is Michael who will descend from the heavens to crush him, and it is he who will set upon him with the sword. And, finally, there are the two sorrows of the kingdom of heaven, Elijah and Enoch, in their earthly bodies among the angels of heaven, awaiting their encounter with Antichrist.

7.STORY OF DAVID

1   David had two famous sons, Solomon and Absalom. Absalom's appearance surpassed that of anyone on earth. The increasing growth of his hair was such that three times its weight in gold was given every year, because his tresses were more beautiful than the gold fringing on royal garments. He was the best horseman in the world. He received land from David after a time. Thereafter David wished to sleep with the wife of his soldier, that is, he desired the wife of the comrade who used to be at his side, though [already] he had fifty concubines. He sent the soldier to his son, Absalom, with a royal message in ogham on his shield urging war on a people opposed to David. The message on the shield was, that once the battle-lines were drawn up, Absalom was to make his escape, leaving the soldier behind, for soldiers would never flee.

2   This was done. Battle was joined. Absalom was defeated. The soldier was left behind. Absalom arrived with news of the battle. David was looking out over the city wall. "Have you tidings, lad?", he asked. "We were defeated and the soldier was left there". "That is bad", said David. "Now I have a remarkable tale to tell" [said Absalom]. "Good", said David. "Two peasants were herding sheep" [said Absalom]. "One of them had a single sheep, while his companion had fifty. The man who had the fifty sheep went and killed the man who had only one sheep. What then should be done to him?" "Indeed he should be stoned to death", said David. "You have passed judgement on yourself", said the lad, "for you have fifty women, and you had your soldier slain for the sake of his only wife".

3   The lad was on his horse. He turned the horse away from him. Thereupon David let fly an arrow. The lad threw himself behind the shelter of a pillar-stone, and the arrow lodged in the pillar. Then David was overcome by regret. He pressed his face to the ground, and remained thus for three days and three nights. It was then that he chanted *Miserere mei Deus secundum magnam*. Now everyone who says the psalm after transgression will have his sin forgiven.

8. THE POWER OF WOMEN

1   There was a famous king of the Greeks called Solomon. A great feast
     was prepared for him by a king from one of his tribes. They all grew
     very drunk. There were untrustworthy persons close to the king. "Let
     me be guarded by you tonight", he told three friends from his [own]
     household. "That will be done", they replied. In this manner they were
     engaged in their watch, with a barrel of wine beside them, and a
     servant holding a candle in their direction. They were all attending to
     each other. "Indeed, it is well for us", said one of the three men. "Let
     us give thanks to our lord. Except in one regard, our bodily senses are
     in a favourable state. The feet rejoice in being stretched out without
     motion. The hands rejoice in dispensing [food] to the body. The eyes
     rejoice in viewing the preparation. Noses revel in the aroma, lips, in the
     taste. One area, however, is not being pleased, and that is our hearing,
     for none of us hears agreeable sayings being passed from one to
     another".

2   The question is put: "What will we discuss?" "Not difficult the reso-
     lution. We will seek to ascertain what power on earth is the strongest".
     "I know", said the Roman warrior. "It is wine. For it is wine which
     intoxicated the host, leaving them without reason or sense, so that they
     were dementedly drunk, cast into sleep, and at the mercy of their
     enemies".

3   "That is a good case", said the Greek, "but it seems to me that the
     stronger power is that of the ruler by whom the wine was given. The
     ruler is stronger than ordinary men, and man is more estimable than
     the rest of creation. It is his power which causes us to be sober and
     sleepless, even though we are drinking wine".

4   "Well", said the Jewish warrior, whose name was Nemiasserus,
     "those were good propositions. Yet it appears to me that the power of
     women is the greatest. It would be no wonder if this is what you
     remember on the morrow". They remained there until the morning.

5   "So now, what judgements were passed among you last night?",
       asked the king. "This one, indeed. We were considering what was the
       greatest power on earth". "I said that it was the power of wine", said
       the Roman. "I said that it was the power of a king", said the Greek. "I
       said that it was the power of woman", said the Jew.

6   The queen was at the king's side. The king himself was wearing his
       golden crown. "Wine is the stronger", said one man. "The power of the
       king is the stronger", said another. "Is it the case that I am without
       power?", asked the queen, striking the king's headgear with the palm
       of her hand, so that [the crown] fell on the floor of the house. "She
       should be put to death", said everyone. The king looked over at her.
       Then the queen smiled. The king immediately smiled too. "No harm
       will be done to the woman", said the king. "There it is, then", said
       Nemiasserus, "that is a mighty power". "It is true", said the king, "the
       power of woman is more powerful than all others. For on her brow is
       her accompanying Satan, so that one cannot reproach her for anything
       she does".

9.THE DEATHS OF THE CHIEF PROPHETS

1 Here follows a discussion of the deaths of the chief prophets, with reference to those responsible for their deaths, and the locations in which the prophets are buried.

2 Manasseh, son of Hezekiah, killed Isaiah, son of Amos, in this way: He had him raised on high, and cleft lengthwise with a hacksaw until he died. He was buried underneath the oak of Rogel.

3 Jeremiah, however, was stoned by the people at Taphnai in Egypt, and he was buried in this same Taphnai, the burial-place of the pharaohs, the kings of Egypt. Thus was the death of Jeremiah, son of Hilkiah of Anathoth.

4 In the case of the prophet Ezekiel, the leaders of the people of Israel killed him on account of the severity of his admonishment, and the extent to which he rebuked them for their sin of impiety. The people buried him in the land of Maour, beside the grave of Arpachshad.

5 The prophet Daniel, moreover, the son of Abda, after he had completed his days in full holiness, he died in the Babylonian captivity. He was buried with honour alone in the royal tomb, for no person had been buried there previously, and nobody was to be buried there afterwards.

THE NEW TESTAMENT

10. INFANCY GOSPEL

1   It was the time and season when stewards and functionaries of the Roman ruler, Octavius Caesar, came to levy the Caesarian tribute. This was the manner in which the tribute was collected. Everyone in the world had to go to his own district to pay it, and it would not be accepted elsewhere. It was called polltax because it was levied on every head of livestock and cattle, on family members and spouses, as well as on wealth, clothing and implements, and all movable and immovable property, both land and produce, held throughout the world. When Joseph (formerly called Moab iustus, because of his righteousness) heard this, he set out with his household, himself and the Virgin Mary, and Simeon, Ameon, and James of the Knees, his three sons, to go from Nazareth in Galilee to Bethlehem of Juda, since that was the city of David, and Joseph had been born there. For Joseph and Mary were of the family of David, there being forty generations exactly between Joseph and David. For that reason, therefore, they went to pay Caesar's tribute to Bethlehem of Juda.

2   When they came near the city Joseph and Ameon went ahead to get lodgings, and Mary stayed behind with James of the Knees and Simeon, for she was very weary after the journey, being close to her time of delivery. It was a four-day journey from Nazareth in Galilee to the city of Jerusalem, with two further days from Jerusalem to Bethlehem of Juda. It was no wonder, then, that the maiden was exhausted after the long trek. And when Joseph reached the centre of the city, great gladness came upon him, and he said: "It is most fitting that everyone should love his native place, and nothing is more appropriate than that everyone should be at ease in his own fatherland ... And my heart is joyous before you, O Bethlehem of Juda, and I am gladdened by the sight of you. You are the heritage which God granted to the noble and honourable patriarch, Abraham. I, however, have come to this city to render tribute to Caesar, and to suffer hardship on that account".

3   Joseph was seated thus on a stone, writing his declaration according to Roman law. This is what he wrote: "I, Joseph, of the city of Bethlehem of Juda, of the tribe of David, am accompanied by the virgin Mary, of the same tribe, who was entrusted to my care by the casting of lots. I am accompanied also by my three sons, Simeon, Ameon, and James of the Knees. I have no wealth save my craftsman's tools. Moreover, the maiden is weary after the journey, and I have come in advance to seek lodgings for her, for she needs a place to stop and rest, where the child in her womb will survive".

4   Then Joseph raised his eyes and saw a certain secluded little house standing alone beside the city, and he said: "We should remain at this house, since it seems to me that it is an abode for visiting strangers". Then Joseph went in and looked around. "It is a small abode", said he, " yet though it be so, it is suitable for poor people. It is remote from the converse and clamour and display of the populace. Stay here, son, while I go to the city to show my wares and fine craftsmanship in the hope of finding someone who will give me something for them".

5   While Joseph and his son were thus conversing together, the voice of the herald was heard proclaiming to the eminent people of the city: "Come, men, and make your declaration without delay, since Cyrinus son of Cirin, chief ruler of the land of Juda, is about to go immediately to confer with the king of the Romans, Octavius Augustus. For that reason, you are to come yourselves with your men and women, your sons and daughters, your male and female servants, your young and old, free and unfree, nobles and commoners. Give a written account of your gold and silver, land and territory, livestock and cattle, clothing and implements, and all your goods besides. Write down your seniority, your debts and your credits, and render justly the tribute of Caesar". James has said that every time this tribute was levied everyone in the whole world had to draw up a will, as if on the point of death, and no man could conceal a penny-worth of his worldly goods from that levy. If he did, everything would be confiscated from him ...

6   As Joseph and Ameon listened to the proclamation, Joseph said to those who were collecting the tribute: "You have given sufficient notice. Everyone who has the wherewithal will pay his tax to Caesar. Come here and see this house", said he, "for it is not really a house at

all, but a small insignificant cave containing a manger for an ass and ox. I see only one bed for the stranger to rest, and one little wooden stool for a guest to sit. These are the property of the owner of the lodging, not mine at all. All I have are my smith's implements, and my craftsman's tools, and though they seem paltry to you in the estimation and reckoning of the tribute, yet they provide a means of livelihood for myself, and for my three sons, and for the maiden whom God sent into my keeping after the drawing of lots, and whom I brought from the great temple of Jerusalem, and from the sons of Israel. These are the only possessions I have".

7   After he had thus paid tribute on behalf of himself, and the four with him, and after the tax-collectors had departed, Joseph remained looking out along the road. In a short while he saw Mary approach the entrance to the city, with Simeon on one side of her, and James of the Knees on the other. Joseph said to his sons: "You were a long time coming, sons". "It is not that we were dilatory", said the sons," but the maiden who is with us is very weary, and every hour and moment of the journey exhausted her, and we feared that she would go into labour before she reached a resting-place".

8   Then Joseph said to Mary: "You have endured much hardship on my account. Come in and rest". "O Simeon", said Joseph, "Bring water and wash the virgin's feet, and give her food and all that she needs, for I am sure that no nobler service has ever been rendered, since the virgin will bear a holy infant known only to the Heavenly Father, the saviour of all, and the creator of every living thing". "O father", said Simeon,"The maiden is speaking, and I do not know whom she is addressing". "I think that she is suffering from tiredness and distress", said Joseph. And when Joseph looked at Mary he saw that she was alternately sad and joyful. "How is it, girl", he said," that at one time you are grieving, while at another time you are happy?"" I see two peoples", said she, " one of which is in mourning, and the other in gladness"...

9   Joseph told her to go to her bed and rest. "O Simeon", said he, "anoint the virgins's feet with oil". Simeon did so, and after Joseph had gone out Simeon followed him, and said:"The virgin is rapidly being overcome by debility, and I think that she will give birth without

delay". "I will not leave her", said Joseph. " Since you are more agile than I am, let you go around the city in search of a midwife for her, for a competent midwife greatly assists a woman in childbirth". "How am I to do that since I know neither the city nor its people?. Yet I will go, for I am sure that God will provide a midwife for her, and everything else that she needs, for He has special concern for her".

10   As they ceased their conversation, they saw a gentle, steady-eyed girl approach swiftly, carrying a chair. "Who are you, girl?", asked Joseph, "and what is the chair which you have?""It is a chair for women in childbirth", said she. "My mistress sent me to bring it to you, and she will follow me herself without delay, for a beautiful handsome youth came to guide us speedily to the virgin who is with you, to assist her in giving birth to the noble king". This amazed them. Joseph looked at the nearby mountain, and saw a tall venerable woman at the summit, vigorously traversing the hill with swift steps until she speedily reached the place in which was the noble senior of Israel, Joseph.

11   As Joseph saw her approach him he went forward to speak to her, and they greeted each other. The woman said to Joseph: "Where are you going?""I am going to seek a Hebrew woman who will attend to the virgin who is about to give birth to the true God and true man, the beneficent king who is the creator of the four elements" said Joseph. "Here I am", said the woman," for I am the best midwife of the Jewish people. Tell me, good man, are you an Israelite yourself?" "I am, indeed", said Joseph. "Who is this young woman brought to a cave lodging?", she asked. "She is married to me", said Joseph. "She is not your wife at all", said she. "She is called the Virgin Mary, she was reared in the temple of the Lord, and it fell to you by lot to look after and protect her". "That is true", said Joseph, "and since the Lord has revealed these things to you, I shall not conceal them. Let us go in to see Mary", said Joseph.

12   When they went to the door of the house they saw a shining bright cloud above the cave, and such was the illumination, both inside the cave and over the outside, that human eyes could not gaze on it. "Enter", said Joseph. "I will", said she," and may the hand of God be with me. And do not show me any disrespect", she said. "For there is no midwife who is my equal throughout the land of the Jews". "We

should rather give thanks to God that through his grace you were found thus", said Joseph. "He who does not esteem God's providence, and does not show gratitude, commits a sin against the Lord". Then Simeon said to Joseph: "You have been blessed, beloved father, and the saints of heaven and the everlasting joy of all joys are with you, and your helper, from the God of gods, the Lord of lords, who is without pride..."

13 The woman went in, and shortly afterwards Joseph followed her. When they came out again Simeon was waiting at the entrance of the cave, and he asked the midwife for news. "Woman", said Simeon, "how is the virgin, and is there hope that she will live?" "I have news, indeed", she said... I bless my God and Lord who revealed these things to me, his servant, unworthy though I am to witness them. And how am I to relate them", said she, "since they are new and extraordinary things, like nothing experienced ever before ?" "I beseech you for the love of God to disclose them to me", said Simeon. "They will not be concealed from you", said she,"for in time, they will be commonly known throughout the whole world , but they have been secret up to now. Heed these words and affix them in your heart, son", she said.

14 "When I came to the place where the virgin was, I saw her praying and blessing the Lord. I asked her if she were in distress of body or mind. She did not answer, but remained immobile as a rock, with her eyes directed towards heaven, praying unceasingly. Then all of creation stood still, the wind ceased its storms, the ocean its roar. The sea was quiet, the wave soundless, the land untraversed, swift-flowing rivers became like pools, streams reposed as if in sleep, fish remained still. There was not a quiver in the woods, leaves were motionless, animals stood at rest, birds did not fly, people could not speak or work during the sacred time while the virgin was giving birth to the everlasting Lord. Assuredly the four elements recognized their creator ... The inhabitants of hell were held fast, motionless and miserable, without the ability to do evil or harm against creature or devout person fashioned by God on that night of the divine birth... "

15 "The virgin was looking upwards, praying constantly ... And we saw a bright light from her shine throughout the cave, so that she was like a single glorious radiance... Many angelic voices were heard above the

cave praising the great Lord, and giving strength to the virgin inside. And the brightness outshone the light of the sun and all the stars. Moreover, a fragrance reached us which would delight everyone everlastingly, with the perfume of all the fruit, wax, saffron, and beautiful ointments in the world, all the herbs and plants and beautiful fruits that ever existed in holy Paradise. More wonderful than all of these, indeed, was the pleasure derived from that fragrance. And heavenly angels were unceasingly in attendance, since there is no human born who could worthily partake of that mystery, except for the Virgin Mary herself".

16   "Deep silence overcame me, and I was seized by fear and terror at the sight of these miraculous events, for the infant was like a sphere of light, such that human eyes could not look on. He was briefly in this form before assuming the shape and appearance of a child, and my mind grew animated as I looked on him, and I bent down and raised him up. He weighed nothing, unlike an ordinary child, and as I examined him attentively, I could find neither blemish nor mark nor trace of blood on him. It was as if he were washed in the gentle beautiful dew of the noble Heavenly Father. No known body was so radiant, no infant so weightless to carry, no human being was ever seen whose beauty was more resplendent. I marvelled that his nature was not like that of any other child, for he did not cry or wail, except for a little as he was being put in the manger. He was without the weakness of infancy, and as I looked in his face, he smiled at me, and no worldly delight was ever as pleasing. The flash of light from his eyes overshadowed the sunlight which reached throughout the cave at dawn from the east ".

17   When Simeon had heard these words he said: "You are blessed and ever-fortunate, O devout and astute woman, and though I am the lowliest, it is propitious for me to have heard of these wonders, though I did not see them. And I believe all that you relate", said Simeon.

11. THE WONDERS OF THE NIGHT OF THE NATIVITY

1   Here are related the seventeen wonders in the world on the night when Christ was born. It was on the eighth day before the calends of January that he was born. Numerous were the miracles and wonders throughout the whole world on that night.

2   On that night the vine was found to have ripened and to be in full fruit in Jerusalem.

3   On that night also, in truth, the palm was found to be bearing its bright crimson flower.

4   On that night twelve ears of clean corn were found in the east of the plain of Bethlehem.

5   On that night fourteen wells gushed from the plains and level lands of Bethlehem.

6   On the same night every lock and chain and fastening, and every temple was found to have opened of its own accord.

7   On that night a great and overwhelming light was seen to enter all the temples of the entire world, and none of those temples shone more brightly under a hot summer sun than they did on that night.

8   This was the seventh wonder, that all the inhabitants of the city were awakened from their sleep and slumber, and it was revealed to them that the sky close by them was full of majestic brightly-shining stars, which illuminated the whole world from east to west.

9   The eighth wonder was that the windows and doors of the great temple of Jerusalem all opened of their own accord on that night.

10   The ninth wonder was that the infants of Bethlehem in their mothers' wombs got the power of speech, as did also the babies who were being

suckled, and all of them were praising the Creator.

11 The tenth wonder was that a well of spring water burst forth in the land of Israel in a place where no well had been before, and this marvel may still be seen.

12 The eleventh wonder was that there was not a plain or field in the land of Juda which was not filled on that night with fiery crimson flowers, all containing honey and luscious fruit.

13 The twelfth wonder was that those with every infirmity were cured. Those who were blind, lame, or deaf, lepers, and those with palsy, were all made well on that night.

14 The thirteenth wonder was that the majestic star gave directions to the magi who came with gifts for Christ of gold, frankincense, and myrrh...

15 The fourteenth wonder was that the beasts and brute animals were awakened from their sleep and slumber, and were praising the Creator in the presence of the hosts, saying in unison with the angels of heaven: "*Sanctus, Sanctus, Sanctus, Dominus Deus Sabaoth*". When the brute unthinking animals adored the Saviour, it behoves human beings to give him unceasing praise forever.

16 The fifteenth wonder was that all the wise men of Bethlehem, both magi and holy sages, were praising Christ in their sleep, and were prophesying concerning his wisdom and great miracles. And this caused great wonder to all.

17 The sixteenth wonder: As the historians relate, there appeared a whale on the shore of the Caspian Sea on that night. Its name was Sem(en)a. Its enormous size was indescribable, for with fifty men on top of its head, and each man distant from another as far as eye could see, such was the extent of land taken up by that whale. There were three hundred and fifty horns on its head, and each horn could hold enough drink for one hundred and fifty. Moreover, the remains [of the whale], and those horns still remain in the houses of nobles in those lands yonder. The written sources say that, when that whale was dying,

three streams gushed forth from his throat, a red stream of wine, a stream of oil, and a stream of red gold.

18 Truly, it was in the time of Octavius Caesar that the prophecies came to pass, and that Jesus Christ was born. For when the Caesarian tax was being levied throughout the whole world, at that time Joseph and Mary came from Nazareth of Galilee to Bethlehem of Juda, to the city of David son of Jesse, for Joseph and Mary were of the line of David, and payment of the tax would not be accepted from them in any other place except in their own paternal land.

11A. ADDITIONAL RELATED TEXT

1 On the day after the birth of Christ, a four-cornered gold ingot appeared in the land of Arabia. From morning to night it continued to grow. The inhabitants of the land and of the adjoining territory were hacking and cutting at it throughout that time, but it remained entirely whole, however much was hewn from it.

2 Now the four-cornered ingot represents the Christian Church throughout the four quarters of the world. The growth of the ingot in the space of a single day signifies the spread of the Church in a single age of the six ages of the world. It also resembles Christ eternally, on whom there will be neither increase nor decrease throughout the ages.

12. THE MAGI

1   On a certain day, as Joseph stood at the entrance to the house, he saw a large group approach him directly from the east. Thereupon Joseph said to Simeon: "Son, who are these drawing near us? They seem to have come from afar". Then Joseph went towards them, and said to Simeon: "It appears to me, son, that they practice druidic augury and divination, for they do not take a single step without looking upward, and they are arguing and conversing about something amongst themselves. I think that they are foreigners, come from distant lands", said he, "for their appearance, colour and attire is unlike that of our own people. They are wearing bright flowing robes, even-coloured crimson tunics, long red cloaks, and variegated gapped shoes. From their apparel they seem like kings or leaders".

2   There were three men in front of the group. One of them was a handsome nobleman, grey-bearded, with high temples. He was called Melcisar, and it was he who gave the gold to Christ. There was another bearded man with very long brown hair. His name was Balcisar, and it was he who gave the frankincense to Christ. Yet another man had fair hair and was beardless. His name was Hiespar, and it was he who gave the myrrh to Christ. Other names for these kings were Malcus, Patifaxat, and Casper. Malcus was the alternate name for Melcisar, Patifaxat for Balcisar, Casper for Hiespar.

3   Joseph said: "Well do they travel, unwearied, though they come from afar". Then they reached the place where Joseph was, along with his son, Simeon. They went past Joseph into the house. Joseph went with them and said: "Tell me, for God's sake, who you are, and from whence have you come to the house without my permission?" "Our leader and lord proceeded us to this small dwelling, and we have followed him", they replied. "From where have you yourselves come?", asked Joseph. "From the east", they said, "from eastern India, the lands of Arabia, the lands of the Chaldeans, and from other various lands in the eastern world".

4   "Why have you come?", asked Joseph. "The answer is not difficult",
     they said. "A king of the Jews, a king of the whole world, has been born
     in this country, and we have come to find him, to do him reverence,
     and to see him"."From whence did you receive that knowledge?",
     asked Joseph. "That is easy", they said. "It has been in our ancient
     books and writings from the time of our first man down to the present
     day that, whenever we should see a star like this one over our land, we
     should go with it whatever way it travelled, because it was a sign of the
     king of the world. For, according to prophecy and foreknowledge, that
     king is destined to save us, and the human race, straight away, after his
     birth".

5   "Why did you not go to Jerusalem to seek him?", asked Joseph. "For
     that is the chief city of the land, where the temple of the Lord is to be
     found. Moreover, the king of the Jews, Herod, dwells there". "We did
     travel there already", they said. "When we reached the city the
     majestic star went away from us, and we did not see it at all. We
     entered the house in which was the king, Herod, and we told him that
     a king of the Jews had been born in his land, and that a regal star had
     proceeded us from the eastern world as far as this place, and had gone
     from us there [in Jerusalem]. Then we inquired of the king, and of the
     Jewish people, as to where he had been born. They said that they did
     not know".

6   "Then all his sorcerers, sages, and men of knowledge and wisdom
     were summoned to Herod, and he asked them where the birth of a
     king of the Jews had been predicted in their prophecies. They all said:
     "In Bethlehem of Juda, as the Holy Spirit declared through the mouth
     of the king, David son of Jesse: *"De diversario in spelonca nasci Christum
     in Bethelem"*..."Then Herod was seized with great trembling and fear,
     and he said: "Where else would a son of a king of the Jews be born but
     in my house?". Then the sooth-sayers said: "It is the son of the king of
     the whole world who was to be born there". Then Herod's mind was
     occupied with many and grievous deliberations and thoughts. The
     wise men of the Jewish people were called back to him, and he
     enquired again attentively as to where, in prophecy or augury, the
     birth of that king was located. They all replied: "In Bethlehem of Juda".

7   Then Herod said to the magi who had come to adore Christ: "Go to

Bethlehem of Juda, and if you find Christ there come back to me, so that I may go myself to adore him. Take my royal diadem to Christ", said he. (This was a royal diadem made of Arabian gold, full of precious stones and ornamented gems. It was, moreover, the diadem which was on Herod's own head every day). "Take with you also for him this royal ring set with conspicuous jewels, the equal or like of which has never been found in the world. It was given to me by the king of Persia. Let you give it to that king yonder, and when you come back, I will go myself to adore him, and bring other gifts for him even better than these".

8   "We brought those gifts with us, then", said the magi, "and we left the city. Immediately after, our own kingly star manifested itself to us, and we rejoiced greatly at that. It proceeded thereafter until it was over this house, above the roof. Then, before our eyes, it entered the house, and you do not allow us to follow in its wake"...

9   Then they asked leave of Joseph to enter the house. Joseph said to them: "I will not keep you from what God himself has revealed to you". Joseph, indeed, would have been pleased if the news were known generally and revealed to all. "A blessing on you", they said. "Let us go now to see the Saviour and God of the people". Then they entered the house, greeted Mary, and said: "*Ave tu benedicta gratia plena*", "God be with you, you who are blessed and full of grace". After that they went to the manger, and beheld Christ there.

10   When the magi had entered the house, Joseph said to Simeon: "Go after them, son, and observe them keenly, in order to see and find out what they do to the child, for it is not my place to watch or scrutinize them". Then Simeon went to keep an eye on them. There were the magi, face downwards, prostrating themselves and bowing down to the Son of God. Simeon was filled with wonder at their behaviour, and related it to Joseph. "Continue to keep watch on what they are doing", said Joseph. They rose up then and opened their gifts, and gave them to Christ. "What have they given him?", asked Joseph. "An easy answer", said Simeon, "gold, frankincense and myrrh, and the presents which Herod gave to them".

11   James of the Knees, the kinsman of Christ himself, says that the magi

gave numerous other gifts to Christ, outstanding purple [gems], shining brilliantly, a bright pearl, a crown of fresh grasses which would never wither, but would bear bright crimson flowers always, a wreath, also, in which were entwined various fresh grasses with crimson flowers, which seemed as if they had just been cut, and a shining new linen cloth, the equal or like of which was not to be found. The latter shone so brightly that people saw flashes of lightning rise from it as from a brilliant star, or as sparks from a mighty fire when its heat is at its most intense. They brought, furthermore, a royal sceptre with gems of crystal and of precious stones, the equivalent or like of which have never been found in the whole of creation from the beginning to the end of the world, except, perhaps, the firmament with [its] many stars, and the sun and moon in it like precious stones. Fire-trailing sparks darted from them as from a brilliant constellation, the brightness of which would make human eyes grow molten. And they gave other gifts, such as were never found in the world.

12   Then Simeon said: "They are good men, and their gifts are reverent. Moreover, they kissed the feet of the infant as they offered their presents to him. They are not like the shepherds who gave him no gifts. For those who gave him gifts, an era of great good will begin, for their descendants will grant gifts forever". That, indeed proved true, for it marked the beginning of the Gentiles' belief in Christ, and the gifts were the first offerings of the Gentiles to God, their first-fruits.

13   Then Joseph said to Simeon: "Observe closely what they are doing now". "They are doing reverence to the boy, and speaking to him", replied Simeon. "I hear their voices, but I do not know what they are saying". "They are all honouring the child", said Joseph. Thereupon the magi came out, and said to Joseph: "O righteous and holy man, you have great good fortune, if you but know it, for the son of the King of heaven and earth is under your fosterage. For we, indeed, have more knowledge of the one who is in your care than you have. The boy who is with you is the God of gods, and Lord of lords, the creator of the elements, the angels and the archangels".

14   "He is the strength and power of God
        He is God's right hand and his wisdom
        He is the controller of the elements and the overseer

of the world
He is the source of death, trembling, and entreaty
for creation
He is judge, physician, and protector of creation
It is he who will summon and disperse the gods
of the Gentiles
It is he who will ravage hell and weaken the
strength and power of the devil
It is he who will destroy the straits of death
It is he who will dissipate the diabolical power
of baleful hell, with its horrible evils
To him all the tribes and races of the whole world
are subject
He is judge and provider for the angels, source of life
for the people of heaven, the protecting breast-plate
of everlasting life, without end or limitation, the
crowning diadem of the heavenly city".

15 Then Joseph said: "From whence did you receive instruction regarding the birth of Christ?" "We became aware of it from our own ancient writings and prophecies, which were foretelling Christ to us long since", said they. "As you enquire about the manner in which we got to know of the birth of Christ, we will relate it all to you from beginning to end, as our fathers and forefathers handed it down to us, from the time of the sons of Abraham to the present day. Now, while we maintained the prophecies and augury which had been left to us, on a certain day, on the calends of January, to be precise, as we were reading the prediction, we suddenly saw the sign which had been recounted to us, a great star, trailing fire, between us and heaven. We were pleased at this, and moreover, nobody else saw it but ourselves alone".

16 "Nobody, unless perhaps an angel of God, could describe that star, its appearance or its colour. For its brightness was greater than the brightness of the sun, and from the day that star appeared to us, its light was greater and more splendid than the light of all other stars and constellations, and such was its brilliance that it filled all heaven and earth. We followed it immediately, as it preceded us with radiance and illumination. It was not wavering or fluctuating like other stars, but

rather it remained evenly and steadily before us without any movement hither or thither. There has not been performed, nor will there be performed, a greater miracle than that the star should thus come from the east of India to the land of Juda, with no guidance, indeed, except the power of God. It then travelled a journey of twelve months in twelve days, higher than a belfry before us. Its mass was equivalent to that of the moon, its light greater than that of the sun".

17   "We followed it on swift horses", the magi told Joseph. "The names of the horses are Dromann Darii, Madian, Effan, and those are the horses which can do a month's journey in a single day, for it is a twelve-month journey from India to the land of Juda. Now the star came in advance of us as far as this place, and stopped over the roof of the house in which is the Saviour. And there is nobody who, on seeing it, would not give all-surpassing love to God, on account of the sanctity and miraculous nature of his covenant".

18   Joseph then asked: "What are your own names?" "That is easily answered. Melcisar is my name", said the grey-bearded man. It is he who gave the gold to Christ. "Balcisar is my name", said the man with the dark-brown beard. It is he who gave the frankincense. "Hiespar is my name", said the young beardless man. It is he who gave the myrrh. Then Joseph said to them: "Now that you have recognized the Creator in the form of a child, come with me to get food and drink, and remain tonight with me. I will buy valuable wine and well-flavoured wheat, and various kinds of edibles for you, because you have believed in the true God, and have given him noble and outstanding gifts".

19   "We must go", they said, "For we have already been satisfied with the heavenly banquet, which is more splendid for us than for you". "It would be good to have an earthly feast as well as a divine one", said Joseph. "We will not stay here tonight, nor will we go to Jerusalem, though we promised to go there", they said, "for [thus] Herod will be the further away from us. An angel came to us last night to tell us to return home by another way, and that is what we propose to do. A blessing on you", they said [to Joseph], "for you are a man chosen by God and held in great honour by him". Thereafter they went home by another route, as the angel had told them.

20   There are various versions of the tidings of the magi in written sources. James of the Knees said in his Infancy Gospel: "Seven was the number of magi, and it was after nine days that they came to Bethlehem of Juda". However, Matthew son of Alphaeus in his gospel, and *in Libro de Infancia Marie,* that is, in the book relating the birth of Mary, says that the magi came after twelve days. Moreover, sacred commentaries say that they were three kings, and that they had sixty ships, and that Herod burned their ships so that they should go to speak to him as they were returning. It is related also that they brought great gifts to Mary and to Joseph, along with those which they gave to Christ.

13. ANECDOTE CONCERNING THE MAGI

1   Iespar, Melcisar, and Balcisar were the names of the magi. This is what is signified by the gifts. Gold was for the royal status of Christ, the frankincense on account of his divinity, the myrrh on account of his humanity. It was the majestic star which guided those magi from the land of Arabia and from the eastern world to the land of Juda, and to Bethlehem, to the house where Christ was, in the stall of an ass and a young ox...

2   When they reached the entrance of the house where Christ was, the elder, Melcisar, entered the house, and the other two remained outside the door, so that their elder could prostrate himself [in reverence], and offer all their gifts. This, indeed, was always their custom, to be submissive to their seniors. Then Hiespar, the youngest, said: "O God almighty, wonderfully fortunate is he who is senior to us today, for it is he who will see the saviour first". When Christ heard that, he transferred the form of the eldest to the youngest, so that that it was the latter who first saw Christ, and who offered his gifts to him before everyone else. And this was one of the first miracles of Christ.

14. INFANCY GOSPEL OF THOMAS

1   When Jesus, son of the living God, was a lad of five years, he blessed twelve little pools of water. He had dammed them with clay.

2   He shaped twelve little birds, called *passeres*. On the Sabbath day he made them firmly from clay.

3   A certain Jew complained about Jesus, son of the great God. He conveyed him by the hand to his foster-father, Joseph.

4   "Rebuke your son, Joseph. What he is doing is not right. On the Sabbath day he fashioned clay images of birds".

5   Jesus clapped his two hands. His small voice resounded. Before their eyes he shooed away the birds - a kingly concession.

6   A gentle endearing little speech was heard from the mouth of faultless Jesus: "So that you may discover who it was who made you, of your own accord, go! ".

7   Someone announced to the people - it was an extraordinary report - that the cries of the birds were heard as they took flight.

8   The son of Annas the scribe came to join Jesus at play. He released each [dammed] stream. He knocked down the constructions.

9   "What you have done has not been to our benefit", said Jesus. "May you be like a little branch which falls before bearing fruit".

10   The boy fell over like a withered twig. It would have been better for him not to have ruined the sport of the King's son.

11   On a further occasion, when Jesus was in Joseph's care, another boy who visited him caused him annoyance.

12 "May the journey which you have made be one of no return", said Jesus. The boy fell over and died straight away.

13 He outraged the kindred of the boy to whom he had dealt doom. Thus they said: "Depart from us, Joseph, with your son. It is time to keep away from us".

14 "If you do not punish your son, go away anywhere. It could not be too soon, whatever path you might take from here".

15 "Why, son, have you offended the people?" asked Joseph. "Anyone on whom you pronounce your judgement is taken away from you dead".

16 "Anyone who is innocent does not die as a result of judgements. It is only the accursed whom the malediction punishes".

17 "It should have been sufficient that I listened to them, and that they met me, without strong men tearing away my two ears from my head".

18 "Your son who does this causes great terror. We have never, until now, heard of any boy like him".

19 "Quicker than a glance, what he says is done forthwith. We have not heard tell of a boy like him in the world".

20 Joseph said: "He is not like everyone else's sons. Even though crucifixion or death were the [expected] outcome, it would not be so for him at all".

21 Everyone who accused him he punished. Deafness affected their ears, and blindness their eyes.

22 The scholar Zacharias said: "This is an amazing boy. If he were to be taught, he would, indeed, be outstanding in learning".

23 Zacharias took him with him to his school, so that he might begin to study with him, like everyone else.

24   When he had written an alphabet for him, he said: "Say *A* ". Though
      the son of the King did not answer him, the amount he knew was
      greater.

25   The master grew angry. He struck him on the head with whatever he
      chanced on, either fist or rod.

26   "It is usual", said Jesus, "that any anvil which is struck teaches
      whoever strikes it that it is not the anvil which is receiving instruc-
      tion".

27   "For what you have taught to all, what you have written for me, the
      letters which you spell out, I know their names".

28   Jesus recited his letters for them before their eyes, each letter with its
      constituent element and its hidden meaning.

29   The scholar Zacharias said: "Take the boy away from me. I do not have
      the means of answering you, lad. Do not provoke me".

30   "I thought that it was a pupil whom I brought with me to my school.
      I saw that it is a master whose charge I had undertaken".

31   "I do not know, in any case, whether he be angel or God. It seems to
      me that until today I proceeded without confusion".

32   "Who is the mother who conceived this infant in her womb? What
      nurse was able to rear this child?"

33   "His patrimony will not be on earth. What is surer is that he is the one
      born to be crucified, who existed even before the Deluge".

34   The boy Jesus replied: "You who are learned in the law of God, you
      think that Joseph is my father. He is not".

35   "I existed before your birth. I am the one who has wisdom. I know
      every secret that has ever been in your heart".

36   "You have sure knowledge of all erudition. You have read everything.

From me you are getting doctrine which is not known to any person".

37 "I have extraordinary news for you, absolutely without falsehood. I have seen Abraham when he was alive".

38 "Likewise, I have seen you a long time ago, through the knowledge of the Holy Spirit. O expert in the Law, I existed at all times before you were born".

39 "This cross which you mention, he who has come for the sake of all, to redeem everyone alive, will encounter it".

40 Once, the sinless son of Mary played a game with boys. His age, as I know, was seven years.

41 One of the boys fell over a cliff and died forthwith. They all fled except Jesus. He waited for a crowd to come.

42 He was accused. It was thought that it was he who had knocked the boy down. "Wait for me", said Jesus, "until I reach him".

43 "I am accused, O Zeno, of laying you low. Is it true?" "It is not true, Lord, not true. Let him go. It is not to be attributed to him".

44 He was dead before, he was dead after, except for when he had said this. When the crowds saw it, they let go of Jesus.

45 His mother sent him for water. Such an amazing boy - he filled an armful of water, and it did not go through his cloak.

46 He sowed a little field with leeks - the amount was not large. When they were harvested subsequently, there were a hundred basketfuls of produce.

47 A piece of craftwork was brought to the house to Joseph to be adjusted, for it projected too far on one side, with one side exceeding the other.

48 Jesus said: "You take hold of your end, and I will take mine. He stretched the shorter side until it was equivalent to the other.

15. THE ABGAR LEGEND

1   Here is the listing of Christ's company, the twelve apostles, as already mentioned. Some of them were namesakes. There were three called James among them, James of the Knees, son of Joseph, James the Great, son of Zebedee, and James *Minor*, son of Alpheus. There were three Simons, Simon Peter, Simon Cannaneus, and Simon Judas Iscariot. There were three called Judas, Judas Thaddaeus, Judas Thomas, and Judas Iscariot. There were two called Thaddaeus, Thaddaeus the apostle, and Thaddaeus the disciple.

2   Now it is this Thaddaeus the disciple whom the apostle Thomas sent to Abgar, king of the land of Armenia and the district north of the river Euphrates. Abgar's leg had become inflamed, and, having heard of the wonders and innumerable miracles of Christ, he sent a letter to Christ.

3   This was its content: *Euagarius filius Came Iesu saluatori qui aparuit in locis Ierusolimorum, salutem.* Now Abgar heard that he healed those suffering from every disease without plant or herb, simply with a word only, and further, that he raised the dead, banished demons, and performed other good deeds besides. And Abgar says to Christ: "You are either of these; you are the God of heaven, earth, and hell, or else you are the son of that God. For this reason I send you a letter, that you may make me well. Now I know that there is much murmuring and plotting against you among the Jews. I have an agreeable little city here, substantial enough for the two of us. So come to us", said Abgar to Christ.

4   Then Jesus wrote the celebrated letter to Abgar: *Beatus es Euagare et cetera* : "Blessed are you, Abgar, to believe in me without having seen me, for many see me and do not believe in me", said Christ. "As you have sent a letter asking me to heal you, first I must fulfil all that I have come on earth to do. Then, when I will go to heaven, you will be healed". Thereafter, Ananias was sent by Jesus to Abgar to say to him: "After the crucifixion and resurrection of Christ, a disciple of mine will

come to you, Abgar. It is he who will make you well". Now after the crucifixion and ascension of Christ, the apostle Thomas sent Thaddaeus the disciple to Abgar to fulfil Christ's promise, and to heal Abgar.

5   At that time Thaddaeus went to the house of Tobias to enjoin faith and piety on him, and to cure every sickness. Abgar was under the impression that he was the man promised by Christ to come to himself to heal him, so Tobias was then summoned to Abgar, who said: "Is it not true that the important man of Christ's household is with you?" "It is true, indeed", said Tobias. "Tell him to come to me", said Abgar. "I will", said Tobias. When Tobias came home, he said to Thaddaeus: "Abgar asks you to go to heal him". "I will go", said Thaddaeus, "as it is for that reason that I came here, to go to him".

6   Tobias set out early on the following morning, along with Thaddaeus, to go to Abgar. As Thaddaeus entered Abgar's house, Abgar saw a shining light and an inescapable radiance emanate from the face of Thaddaeus, so that all the walls of the house were lit up by it. When Abgar saw him, he immediately bowed his head before him. All were astonished at the homage shown by Abgar to Thaddaeus. "Truly you are Christ's own disciple", said Abgar. Thaddaeus said: "It is I who was promised to you. If you wish for true faith, and persevere in it, I will make you well". Abgar said: "I have believed, and I do believe. And if I had been beside Christ with my hosts when the Jews crucified him, I would have killed and slaughtered them, unless the might of the Romans had been alongside them". "It was in accordance with his own will, and the will of the heavenly Father that he was crucified ", said Thaddaeus. "I believe that they are both God, unique and almighty", said Abgar.

7   Then Thaddaeus laid his hand on Abgar, and healed him instantly. Abgar marvelled greatly that, with only a word, Thaddaeus healed the disease in his leg, despite the extent of its virulence and malignancy. And he healed many others besides.

16. LETTER OF JESUS ON SUNDAY OBSERVANCE

1   Here begins the Epistle of the Saviour, our Lord Jesus Christ, concerning Sunday. His own hand wrote it in the presence of the inhabitants
of heaven, and it was placed on the altar of the apostle Peter in Rome
of Latium in order to have Sunday kept holy for all time. When this
epistle was brought from heaven the whole earth began to tremble
from east to west, and the land heaved up its stones and trees in fear
of the Creator, and in joy at the visitation of the angels who came with
the Epistle. Such was the rumbling that the Roman grave of the body
of the apostle Peter opened at that time. While the abbot of Rome was
offering Mass, he saw the Epistle on the altar.

2   It was found to contain this: "People should be prohibited from
transgressing Sunday. For whatever plague or suffering appeared in
the world, it came because of non-observance of Sunday. In some
eastern regions there are beasts sent to men as punishment for neglect
of Sunday. These are called *brucha*, with iron spikes in place of hair,
and fiery eyes. They enter the vineyards, cut the tendrils of the vine,
and make them fall on the ground. Then they roll about on the fruit,
so that the grapes become impaled on their spikes, and they bear them
away thus to their lairs".

3   "There are also other creatures such as locusts there. These have iron
wings, which fasten around everything they encounter. They go in
amidst the wheat, and fasten on the ears of corn until they fall to the
ground. This, indeed, is to punish people for violation of the Sunday".

4   It is commanded by the heavenly Father in the Epistle to show mercy
to the poor and infirm, and to pilgrims. The tears which these shed
when faced with inclemency are visible on the Creator himself. It is he
who avenges the wrong done to them.

5   This is the order from heaven, that Sunday be observed from eventide
(vespers) on Saturday to the end of Monday morning (tierce on

Monday). Christ, son of the living God, who endured crucifixion and martyrdom on behalf of the human race, rose from the dead on Sunday. Even on that account alone, Sunday should be exalted. On that day, moreover, he will come on Doomsday, to judge the living and the dead. It is advisable for all to be in readiness for it. It is there that all will be judged justly, in accordance with the magnitude or smallness of their offence. "He who does not keep Sunday for its proper purposes, his soul will not attain heaven", says the heavenly Father. "Neither will he look on me, nor on the archangels and apostles, in the kingdom of heaven".

6   "Any horse which is ridden on Sunday becomes a horse of fire under the thighs of his rider in hell. Any ox, or servant, male or female, who is kept in wrongful subjection on Sunday, sheds tears of blood from the eyes to God, because God gave them that day as a day of freedom. For not even those in hell are tortured on that day".

7   "Unless you observe Sunday within its proper limits", says the Lord, "there will come on you great storms, many fiery lightning flashes, thunder and lightning which will burn families and peoples, heavy, stony hail-showers, and flying serpents. Heathens will come to you through my agency", said God himself. "A race of pagans will bring you from your own lands into captivity, and will sacrifice you to their own gods. There are, moreover, five huge, horrible beasts in the depths of hell seeking a way to come on earth to people to punish their neglect of Sunday, unless the mercy of God holds them back".

8   "This is the reward for those who keep Sunday holy: The windows of heaven will be opened for them, and God will grant a blessing on themselves, on their dwellings, and on their lands, so that no poverty or hunger will affect a house in which Sunday is observed. Any prayer asked of God at the burial-places of saints will be granted to those who maintain Sunday observance. They will inherit the earth here, and they will have heaven in the next life, and the Lord will make welcome their souls".

9   "If you do not keep Sunday holy", says the Lord, "I swear by my power, and by the only-begotten Son, Christ son of God, and by my holy angels, that fire will rain down on you on the feast of John, killing

everyone, men and boys, women and girls, and your souls will be in everlasting hell thereafter".

10   "This is what I forbid", God says: "On Sunday, let there be neither dispute, controversy, law-case nor contention, no trading nor horse-driving. There shall be no sweeping the floor of a house, no shaving, washing or bathing, no grinding in mill or quern, no cooking, churning or spinning, no conjugal intercourse, no travelling beyond boundaries, no swift running, casting shots, or riding on horse or ass, nor anything which is criminal. Anyone who does such a thing on Sunday, unless he greatly repents of it, his soul will not attain heaven".

11   "I swear by the power of God the Father, and by the cross of Christ", said the abbot of Rome, "that this is not a product of my imagination, nor it is a fiction or fabrication, rather, it is from God the Father that this letter was brought to the altar of Peter in Rome of Latium, to render Sunday holy. Even if there had not come from Jesus Christ himself this wondrous precept for the observance of Sunday, the day should be sacred, revered, sanctified, and honoured, since it was the day on which all these miracles happened".

12

a   "For it was on a Sunday that the first light of day ever in the world was seen.

b   On a Sunday God first created heaven and earth, and, on the first Sunday, the formless primordial matter, and angelic light.

c   On a Sunday God allowed Noah's ark to come to rest on the mountain of Armenia after its escape from the torrent of the deluge.

d   On a Sunday a rainbow appeared as a sign of the saving of Adam's seed after the deluge, for God had promised them that when the rainbow was to be seen his anger would not descend.

e   On a Sunday the Israelites crossed the Red Sea dry-shod.

f   On a Sunday God provided the heavenly food for the Israelites, the pleasant manna, when they were forty years in the desert.

g   It was on a Sunday that the son of God the Father was conceived in the womb of the virgin Mary, not by male agency, but by the grace and inspiration of the Holy Spirit.

h   On a Sunday he was born of the Virgin, whose virginity was not diminished either by the birth or thereafter.

i   On a Sunday, the child was venerated by three magi who came to him with their triad of gifts, gold, frankincense, and myrrh.

j   On a Sunday the Son [of God] was baptized by John the Baptist in the river Jordan.

k   On a Sunday Christ blessed the five loaves and two salmon, so that five thousand were fed from them, and they had twelve baskets of leftovers.

m   On a Sunday, the transfiguration of the divinity and humanity of the Son of God on Mount Tabor, to which these five were witnesses: Peter, John, and James, from the people of this earth, Moses, from the dead, and Elias, from the sanctified.

n   On a Sunday, he (Christ) rode on the ass, when palms were strewn before him.

o   On a Sunday Christ overcame the demon, on the fifteenth of February.

p   On a Sunday was the first preaching of Christ himself in the temple, on the Kalends of May.

q   On a Sunday Christ made wine from water in Canaan of Galilee, at the wedding of John, the beloved disciple.

r   On a Sunday the extraordinary vision and heavenly revelation was seen by John son of Zebedee, that is, the mystical Apocalypse .

s   The resurrection of the Lord was on a Sunday.

t   On a Sunday, Christ himself came forth from the enclosed captivity in which he was placed by the Jews, without opening a lock or chain.

u   On a Sunday he bestowed on his disciples [mastery of] the many languages on earth.

w   On a Sunday the Holy Spirit descended on the apostles in the form of fire.

x   On a Sunday will be the general resurrection, when Christ will come to judge the living and the dead.

y   On a Sunday all created things will be renewed in a better and more beautiful form than they were fashioned in their first creation, when the stars of heaven will be like the moon, the moon like the sun, and the sun like the brightness of seven suns, as was the first light of the sun, before the sin of Adam.

z   On a Sunday Christ will separate the two groups, the innocent lambs, the saints and the just, being separated from the host of arrogant sinners of the world.

13   Therefore, by these precepts God commanded that the sanctity of Sunday be maintained, because the hand of God himself wrote that commandment for people, that they should not perform any business or servile work on a Sunday".

17. THE MYSTICAL TREE

1 Learned tradition tells of a wonderful tree, with its upper part above the firmament, its lower part in the earth, and every melody in its midst. Another of its marvellous features was that was that it grew downward from above, while every other tree grows upward. It grew downward from a single root, with innumerable roots coming from it below. There were nine branches, every branch more beautiful than that above. There were pure white birds on the forks of the branches, listening to their many melodies throughout the ages.

2 The tree is Jesus Christ, the acme of all God's creatures, above them by reason of his divinity, who came forth on earth, assuming humanity from the Virgin Mary. All the melody in the tree's midst represents the perfection of every bliss in the mystic depths of the divinity. It grew from above, that is, from the Heavenly Father. Its single root from above is the one Godhead of the divinity. The many roots below are the twelve apostles, the disciples, and the saints. The nine branches are the nine heavenly orders, with each order more noble than that before it. The white birds among the branches are the shining souls of the just among the heavenly orders.

3 Those of us who dwell together here implore the mercy of God that we may dwell among the branches of that tree, that is, among the heavenly orders.

18. THE DEATH OF JOHN THE BAPTIST

1   There was a wicked and cruel king in the eastern world, Herod son of Antipater, who was responsible for the killing of John the Baptist. This is the reason why the outstanding and noble young man was killed: There was a good judge in Herod's kingdom, who made just decisions and arranged equitable peace terms among all the various peoples, and proclaimed their rights and their laws to them. His name was Philip, a man of great justice and good fortune. Ardargas was the name of the city where he dwelt. And disease came upon him, and within a short time he died. He had a beautiful graceful wife who had few equals in the whole world for comeliness and shapeliness, eloquence, and artistic skill. Even while her own husband, Philip the judge, was alive, Herod loved her greatly, and he often thought of taking her away by force, but for the power of the man with whom she lived.

2   Now when the king of Ascolon, Philip son of Antipater, the brother of Herod, heard that Herodias the wife of Philip was without a husband, he hurried with a host to the place where Herodias was, and took her away with him. She cohabited with him as his spouse for a long time. Herod's heart was seized with great jealousy and insupportable ferocity because the woman he loved most in the world had been taken from him by his own brother. And because of his intense love for her, he did not allow any change in his feelings, despite the fact that she remained with his brother.

3   Thereafter the king gathered together a large troop, and came to Ascolon as if on a royal circuit. He reached his brother's dwelling, and Philip rose to greet him, kissed him and made him welcome. He assigned him a lodging-house that was fittingly prepared, and he served Herod with plentiful food and drink. When his meal ended Herod rose up furiously, having many of his armed and equipped soldiers with him, as he had previously arranged, and he proceeded in that fashion to the house in which Herodias and Philip were. Herod had no weapon except a big pliant rod. When he entered thus, he

found himself at a beautiful princely throne, with the lustre of gold on its joists. Philip was upon it, with Herodias beside him. Herod was enraged throughout his whole being, and he raised his hand, and struck Philip on the crown of his head with a reckless blow from his rod.Then he dragged him from the throne, interposed himself beside Herodias and kissed her. His brother's bed was prepared for him, and he brought the woman there, and slept with her that night. Next day he took her with him to his own city, and thereafter she was his paramour.

4   When John the Baptist, son of Zacharias, heard these tidings, he was displeased that Herod should have taken a concubine. There was, indeed, close kinship between John and Herod, because Cassandra daughter of Gomer was the mother of Herod and Philip, while Elizabeth, another daughter of Gomer, was the mother of John the Baptist. John urged Herod to repudiate the woman, and came often to Herod to say this. In fact, she was the first unlawful spouse ever denounced in the world. Furthermore, John himself was the first martyr in Christendom, as well as the first hermit, the first monk, and the first believer. He was outstanding as a prophet among prophets, a hermit among hermits, a confessor among confessors, a celibate among celibates, and as an apostle among apostles. For he it is whom the Lord well described thus: "Among all the women's sons in the world none has been born who is greater than John the Baptist".

5   Herod then came to the land of Juda, and a great feast was prepared by him there. Herodias, Herod's woman, had two daughters. Sailusa and Neptis were their names. One of the girls was a singer, a flute-player, and a performer of various kinds of music. The other, more-over, was adept at acrobatics, leaping, and gymnastics. Herod brought them into the house to urge them to perform their arts, and to delight the spirits of the nobles and great lords of the world who were gathered within. The girls said that they would not perform unless they received whatever they desired. The king promised this to them, and they bound him to his word in the presence of all the assembled nobles that he would fulfil whatever demands they made on him.

6   Then, after that, they displayed their wonderful talents with skill and energy, and the dignitaries present praised their art highly. When they

had finished their performance they came to their mother, Herod's concubine, to consult her regarding the demand which they would make on the king. "Ask for the head of John the Baptist, and do not accept any other offer but that, and have the head brought to you on a platter", said the queen. The girls came to Herod and asked him for John's head. Herod was displeased at this, and said that he would sooner give them the greater part of his kingdom and territory than to give them the head which they were seeking. But they persisted, and since he had given them his word as king that he would fulfil his undertaking, he conceded to them that John's head should be struck off.

7   Thereafter John the Baptist was beheaded, and the head was brought in on a platter on the head of one of the women. It is said, moreover, that there was nobody to be found to behead John until the Irishman Mog Ruith did so for the sake of the payment involved. As a result of this, cold, hunger, and disease have been inflicted in greater measure on the Irish than on all others.

8   Herod was distressed at the deed because he feared the reaction of the people to the beheading of John. The head was given to Herodias thereafter, and John's disciples sought the body for burial. This was granted to them, and it was buried with respect. Herodias, however, buried the head without revealing the location to John's disciples or friends. On a certain occasion, a long time afterwards, two holy monks from the eastern world came to Jerusalem to fast in honour of the Lord. An angel met them on the way, and said to them:" There is a house in Jerusalem in which is the head of John the Baptist. I will show you where it is. Let you take the head away from there". The monks reached Jerusalem, went to the place which the angel pointed out to them, and took the head with them. Its complexion and appearance were still as good as they had been when the head was attached to the body. They placed it in a satchel of theirs in order to bring it with them to their own land.

9   As the monks set out on the journey towards their fatherland, they encountered a certain man on the way. He was a skilled craftsman who had left his own homeland because of poverty. The monks put the satchel containing John's head on his back. They proceeded then to a

certain city which was on their route, and spent the night there. John the Baptist appeared to the craftsman that night and said to him:" I am John the Baptist, and it is my head which is in the satchel on your back. Rise up, leave the monks, take the head with you, and you will receive food and clothing [through its power]", said he. The artisan arose and left the monks, taking with him the satchel containing the head.

10 He came to the city called Inshena, and remained there for a time. He was greatly honoured and regarded in that city, and people trusted him. Thereafter the craftsman fashioned a golden shrine around the head. This could be shut and opened, and it had a lock on it. Now the craftsman died subsequently, and he left his dwelling to his sister, a pious widow. When she died, she bequeathed the shrine to her heir. However, another man called Eodraissimus took the shrine which contained the head. Many wonders and miracles were performed for him by virtue of his having the head, and diseases and pestilences among the people were cured. The marvels and miracles of John the Baptist were thereby spread abroad.

11 When tidings of the man [who had the head] became known, however, he was banished from the district. A holy man called Marcellus took his place in the house where he lived. Inside that house was the head of John the Baptist, which had been concealed in the ground. John appeared in the night to Marcellus, and told him that the head was buried under the house. He pointed out where the head was, and told him to unearth it. When Marcellus heard this, he told the bishop, Lubrabanu[s], who ruled over that particular city, Emisena. The bishop came, together with the people of the city, and they raised John's head out of its burial-place. They sang psalms and hymns in honour of John, and everyone rendered praise to him, since they had seen all the miracles which the head had performed daily, the head of the chaste martyr, John the Baptist.

19. GOSPEL OF NICODEMUS

(Prologue)

In the nineteenth year of the reign of Tiberius Caesar, emperor of the Romans, and high king of the whole world, in the same year in which the son of Herod was king over the Jewish people and the children of Israel, on the twentieth day of March of that year, an innumerable host of Jews came to denounce and accuse Jesus Christ, son of the living God in the presence of the man called Pilate. The latter was a judge and justiciary, the man who administered law, rule, and the maintenance of right among the Jewish people on behalf of the high king of the Romans, Tiberius Caesar.

I

1   These were the leaders of the group who came to make the aforementioned denunciation: Annas and Caiaphas, two high priests of the Jews, Nicodemus, Abime, Dathan, Gamaliel, Judas, Leui, Neptalim, Alexander, Sirus, as well as the rest of the Jews. This is what that group said to Pilate: "There is a conspicuous person in the land who is leading the people astray with false teaching. He is a son of Joseph, a craftsman, and Mary is his mother's name. His own name is Jesus. Furthermore, he disrespects and defiles our Sabbath, and banishes and breaks our ancestral law". Pilate asked: "Show how he breaks the law". They answered: "One of the fundamentals of the law is not to work on the Sabbath, that is on a Saturday. Yet it is on that day that Jesus Christ healed certain people who were blind, deaf, lame, or hunchbacked, lepers, and those who were agitated by demons, or by reason of various other diseases". "It would seem to me", said Pilate, "that the man who did those deeds should be praised rather than condemned". "No", said they, "for he is a diabolic person, who cures everyone by demonical power". "It is not at all likely", said Pilate, "that it is through an unclean spirit that he banishes those demons from the places which they are wont to frequent. Rather, it appears

more probable that it is through the efficacy of God that he could order the demons to leave their haunts".

2   "We beseech you, O lord Pilate", they responded, "that through your dignity and sovereignty you have this man brought before you, so that you may speak to him". Then Pilate sent Cursor, a messenger, to ask Jesus to come and speak to him. The messenger went to the place where Jesus was, and he did him homage, and bowed down before him. He spread the garment which he was wearing on the ground before Jesus Christ, saying to him: "O Lord, go to the judgement-chamber, for Pilate seeks you".The Jews saw the honour which the messenger showed to the Saviour, and they rose up, saying: "O lord Pilate, why was it not by means of the shout of the herald or steward that you summoned that corrupter into your presence? Why did you sent Cursor to fetch him with honour?" They then told him of the homage which the messenger showed to Jesus.

3   Pilate called the messenger, and enquired why he had shown reverence to Jesus, and why he had honoured him. The messenger replied: "O lord, on a former occasion when you sent me to Jerusalem, I saw Jesus Christ riding on an ass. The Jewish youths were spreading their garments beneath his feet, and, with palm branches in their hands, they bowed down to reverence and honour Jesus. They cried out to him: "Save us, O Lord, O son of God who has come to our assistance".

4   At that, the Jews again cried out together against the messenger, saying: "How did you understand their Hebrew language, since you yourself are a Greek?" The messenger answered: "I had a companion who was Hebrew, who revealed to me everything that they were saying in their own tongue". Pilate said: "The messenger has not transgressed at all in doing reverence to Jesus, since he saw a host of the Jews themselves act thus". Pilate said to the messenger: "Go and bring that same man to speak with us". The messenger did as he was told, and asked Jesus to go to Pilate, as respectfully as he had done before. The latter was in the court-room, and before him were his soldiers, holding standards aloft on staffs.

5   And when Jesus entered the palace, the staffs which bore the standards bowed down forcibly in the soldiers' hands, through the mir-

acles of God, when Jesus came into their presence. Yet the Jews rebuked the soldiers who were holding the standard-poles. The soldiers, however, said that they had bowed down the standards involuntarily.

6   Pilate said: "It is not a matter to be adjudicated at all whether the banners bowed down against their wishes, and adored Jesus". " It was not the standards that did obeisance, but those who were holding them" [said the Jews]. "Let Jesus go out again, and let twelve outstand-ingly strong soldiers hold the standards to see if they will bow again, as before". The standard-bearers got up, and Jesus went out again, and when he entered the palace a second time, the standards bowed down over their hands, and did homage to Jesus.

II

1   When Pilate saw that miracle, he set about rising from his chair, and installing Jesus there, for he was filled with great fear and terror. Just at that time a messenger came from his wife to Pilate, telling him: "Decide justly the case of the holy man who is before you, for I suffered much anxiety and torment last night on his account". The Jews responded by saying to Pilate: "We have told you, Pilate, that man is devilish, and now his evil-doing is manifest, for he sent a demon as a tempter to harm your wife".

2   Pilate then called Jesus to him, and said: "Do you hear the grievous accusations which this crowd make against you? Why do you not reply to them?" Jesus answered calmly, and said to them: "If they did not have the power of speech, they would not speak, but from the day that God granted them the ability to use their tongues, they can proclaim either good or evil, and the end result of this will eventually be manifest".

3   The elders of the priests and the Jews replied, saying: "We observe, and we know from the beginning, that it was through an illicit union that you were conceived, for your mother and father were not married. We know, furthermore, that it was in Bethlehem you were born, and

that, as a result of your birth there, a terrible slaughter was visited on the country, with the killing by Herod of the other children in his search for you, all the boys between the age of two, and the age of a year and a day. We know a third fact, moreover, that your father and mother fled with you from Jerusalem to the land of Egypt, because they did not dare to remain in their own country on your account".

4   Then a large group of Jews who had not participated in the accusation of Jesus said: "We do not concur that he was conceived in an illicit union, for we know that Joseph was married to Mary". Pilate said to the Jews who were denouncing Christ: "It seems to me that what you relate of that man is not true, for a host of people of your own race is contradicting you, and saying that Jesus is the son of a married couple". Then Annas and Caiaphas, along with all the people who were denouncing Christ said: "It is we who are truthful, and not those people. Those who oppose us are disciples of Jesus. They are aliens in our land, and cannot lawfully be accepted as witnesses against us". Pilate asked Annas and Caiaphas: "Who are these people who are siding with Jesus?" "They are pagans", they told him, "who had Jewish mothers, and thus call themselves Jews". These were the names of the twelve men who affirmed that Jesus was born of a wedded mother: Lastair, Astair, Antoin, Jacob, Tetos, Samuel, Isaac, Fineis, Crispus, Agrippa, Ames, Judas. These said: "We are not aliens, but are of Jewish ancestral descent, and we speak the truth, for we were present at the marriage of Joseph and Mary".

5   Pilate said to the foregoing twelve: "I beg of you that you give your oath on this, that you may swear in the house of Caesar that he is the son of a wedded wife". These said: "We have a law against taking an oath in any worldly assembly. Let the others swear that we are telling a lie. We are prepared to risk our lives". Then the accusers of Jesus answered: "We believe those twelve when they say that he was born of a wedded mother. Nevertheless, he is a diabolical person, since he proclaims himself to be the son of God, and a king as well. We do not believe in him".

6   Pilate ordered all the Jews to be sent out of the palace, except the twelve men who had given testimony on behalf of Christ, and Jesus Christ himself. He asked why the Jews were demanding the death of Christ.

They answered that it was because of envy and malice, and on account of the many miracles which he had performed among the people. "It seems to me", said Pilate, "that it is because of his good deeds that they wish harm on him".

III

1   Then Pilate went angrily out of the palace, and said: "I call sun and moon to witness that I do not find any reason for death, nor, indeed, any crime or sin against the holy man yonder". The Jews replied, saying: "If he were not an evil man, we would not have handed him over to you". Pilate responded angrily and vehemently: "Take him with you, and judge him according to your own law". The Jews said: "We cannot put someone to death unless you give judgement that he merits the penalty of death".

2   Pilate went into the palace again, called Jesus to him, and said: "Are you the king of the Jews?" Jesus answered him: "Do you say this of your own accord, or has someone else told you?" Pilate replied, saying: "You see that I am not a Jew, and that it is your own Jewish race which has delivered you into my hands. What have you done against them?" Jesus answered, and said: "My ancestral kingdom is not in this world. If it were, my people, and my own household would have fought on my behalf, and the Jews would not have handed me over". Pilate said: "So you are a king, then?" "You say that I am a king, and you tell the truth, for it is for that I was born, and for that I came. And everyone who is on the side of truth should listen to me". Pilate said: "The law proclaims that truth is not to be found on earth". "That is false", said Jesus, "for there will be truth on earth for as long as I am on it".

IV

1   Then Pilate left Jesus in the palace, and went out himself. He told the Jews that he had not found any fault or crime in Jesus, and that no harm ought to to be done to him. The Jews said: "He has done evil for which

he deserves to die, for he said that he would demolish the temple of God, and rebuild it in three days". Pilate asked: "To what temple was Jesus referring?" "The temple which Solomon son of David took forty-seven years to build, yet Jesus said that he would build it in three days". Pilate said: "I call heaven and earth to witness that I am not guilty of the blood of this holy man". However, the Jews replied: "His blood be upon us , and upon our sons after us".

2   Then Pilate called the elders, priests, deacons and noblemen of the Jews to him, and told them: "I do not find crime, sin, or fault in the man whom you denounce to me as one deserving of death". The elders of the Jewish priests said to Pilate: "We all affirm that everyone who practices deceit should die, and he has deceived his lord".

3   Pilate ordered the Jews to go out of the palace, and he called Jesus to him, and asked: "What am I to do with you?" Jesus replied: "From the earliest times, Moses, son of Amra, and the prophets foretold my coming and my resurrection". The Jews rose up against Jesus, and said: "What greater falsehood could we assert against him than that which he himself asserts?"

4   Pilate said : "If his testimony to me is false, take him, and judge him according to your own laws". "According to the law", said Judas, "if a person offends against his neighbour, he should give the neighbour restitution to the value of forty talents less one. If he offends against God, however, he should be stoned immediately".

5   Pilate looked at the Jewish crowd, and seeing a large group sorrowing and lamenting greatly that Jesus was in captivity before them, he said: "Not all the people are complaining about Jesus, and demanding his death". The Jews answered and said: "We have come here to see that he should die, and that his name should be set down as a lesson to the people". Pilate asked: "Why does he deserve to die?" They answered that it was because he had proclaimed himself the son of God. "Then let him be executed without delay", said Pilate.

V

1   Then a noble Jew called Nicodemus rose up before Pilate and said :
     "Hear me, O lord, Pilate, and allow me a few words with you". "Speak,
     and I will listen", said Pilate. "I ask of the nobles, priests, and deacons,
     and of the whole Jewish people why they seek the death of Jesus. For
     there has not come, nor will there come, anyone amongst the Jews able
     to perform such wonderful signs and miracles as did Jesus. For this
     reason I offer bold but godly counsel to the aforementioned people,
     that they free Jesus from the charges against him. If his manifold deeds
     are performed through the power of God, they will truly prosper. If,
     however, they come from the devil, they will perish, like every
     falsehood".

2   The Jews replied to Nicodemus in fury and anger : "We believe you to
     be a disciple of Jesus because you are speaking on his behalf".
     Nicodemus responded : "Pilate is no disciple of Jesus, yet he who is
     appointed by Caesar as his representative amongst you, Jews, speaks
     on behalf of Jesus". The Jews snarled and bared their teeth at Nicode-
     mus because of those words, and they said: "May his truth and power
     avail you and your soul in the hereafter". Nicodemus answered : "So
     be it, as you have said".

VI

1   Then another nobleman of the Jews leapt up, and asked for a hearing
     from Pilate, who agreed. "For a full year", said the man, "I lay ill in bed,
     unable to rise, and I asked my servants to bring me to Jesus. When he
     saw me, his mercy came upon me, and he said to me: ' Rise up and
     walk'. And I rose immediately afterwards at the word of Jesus, and I
     am to this day without illness or ill-health". The Jews asked that man:
     "On what day were you healed?" He replied that it was on the
     Sabbath, that is, on Saturday. "Is this not what we told you, O lord,
     Pilate?", said the Jews, "that it was on the Sabbath that he performed
     all his healings"?

2   Thereupon another Jewish man got up, and said : "I was born blind,
     and heard the voice of Jesus though I did not see him. I prayed that his

mercy would descend on me. Then he put his fingers over my eyes, and immediately I saw him". Yet another man rose, and said : "I was hunchbacked from birth, and he cured me with a single word". A further man rose, and said : "I was a leper, and he cured me with a single word".

VII

Then a Jewish woman got up, saying: "I had a haemorrhage for twelve years, and I caught and applied to me the hem of his garment, and straight away the flow of blood was stopped". The Jews responded : "It is in the law that the testimony of a woman be not accepted".

VIII

Then there rose together a large crowd of Jews, both women and men, who declared that never before had come a prophet such as Jesus, to whom all the demons were in subjection. Pilate asked the Jews : "Why are the demons not in subjection to your teachers as they are to Jesus?" "We do not know", they replied. Now another group of Jews proclaimed how Jesus had resurrected Lazarus after four days and nights in the grave. Pilate trembled from from head to foot, and said : "O people, what does it profit you to take innocent blood?"

IX

1   Then he called to him Nicodemus, and the twelve men who were assisting Christ, and said : "What am I to do, for much evil counsel has been set before the people?" "We are aware of that", they replied. "You shall see how they shall be punished for it". Thereupon Pilate called all the Jewish people to him, and said to them : "You know that it is an ancestral custom among you that at every great festival a prisoner condemned to death is set free without ransom or punishment, by judgement of the law. There are at present two prisoners in my charge, Barabbas, as a murderer, and Jesus Christ, who is guilty of no crime or sin. Make your choice as to which of them you wish to be

freed from my power". The Jews rose together, saying : "Let Barabas be freed, and let Jesus be crucified". And they declared : "If you let Jesus go free, you will be no friend of Caesar, for everyone who proclaims himself a king is an enemy of Caesar. Now Jesus says that he is the son of God, and that he is a king. For that reason Jesus must not be freed, for, after all, you yourself are the servant of Caesar".

2 Pilate grew furious at this, and said to the Jews : "Truly you are an envious, odious people. You are turning upon the one who comes to your own assistance". The Jews responded, saying : "Against whom have we turned thus?" Pilate replied : "Against your own God, he who freed you from terrible captivity in Egypt, and brought you dry-shod across the Red Sea, as though you were traversing across land. It is he who fed you in the desert with manna, that is, with the bread of angels, and satisfied your thirst with water drawn from fortress of stone. He gave you your ancestral law, brought you to faith, and guided you in every way. After all that, you betrayed and defied your Lord, adoring the golden calf made by human hands, and forsaking your own God. Because of this deed, your God was on the point of exterminating you all, until Moses prayed on your behalf that you should not all die together. Since you acted thus at that time, it is no wonder that you should tell me that I hate my own king and lord".

3 Then Pilate got up from his royal seat, wishing to leave, but the Jews rose, and said : "Though you may leave, it is Caesar who is king over us, and not Jesus. Moreover, it is on account of Jesus that Herod killed the boys in Bethlehem when he heard that the Midian wise men had brought him gifts as though for a king". When Pilate heard those words, he became afraid and fearful, and in the hearing of all the people he cried out : "Is it the case that this is the Jesus whom Herod was seeking?" They all answered that it was so.

4 Then Pilate got water, and washed his hands before the people, saying : "I am innocent of the blood of this righteous man". The Jews replied : "Let his blood be upon us, and on our sons after us". Then Pilate ordered that Jesus be brought into his presence, and he delivered judgement on him in these words : "O Jesus", said he, "Your own people made accusation about you to me, affirming that you proclaimed that you were a king, and that you were the son of God. For

this reason, I hand you over to the control of these people, in accordance with the judgement of the law, to be scourged, beaten, and battered first, and thereafter to be crucified".

X

1   Then Jesus was dragged out of the palace, and there were two thieves along with him, called Dismus and Iasmus. When they reached the place of crucifixion, Jesus was strippped of his garments, and a crown of thorns was placed on his head. He was then crucified, with the two thieves on either side of him, namely, Dismus at his right side, and Iasmus at his left. Jesus said : "O father, spare and forgive the wretches who are doing this, for they do not know what they are doing". Then the Jews divided Christ's garments among them by the casting of lots, and those Jews who were around the cross were deriding Jesus, saying : "If you are the son of God, save yourself now". The leaders and elders of the Jews, moreover, were saying amongst themselves after them : "He saved others, and is not able to save himself. If he be the son of God, let him come down from the cross, and we will believe in him". Then Jesus said : "I am thirsty". Thereupon the soldiers filled a vessel with vinegar and gall, and gave it to Jesus, who drank it. Then one of th soldiers whose name was Longinus came forward. His apppearance was such that his face was a flat surface, and he was without eyes. With a great spear he struck Jesus's side, as he had been instructed, for no-one who could see Jesus wished to wound him. Immediately there flowed two streams from Jesus's side, a stream of blood, and a stream of water. And Longinus rubbed on his forehead the blood which ran down his spear. Then two clear grey eyes appeared in his head, and when he thus saw the face of Jesus he believed in him, and asked his mercy. This was immediately granted to him. Pilate then ordered that an inscription be placed above the head of Jesus on the cross, written in Hebrew and Greek and Latin. This is what was written : "Here is the king of the Jews". The Jews rose up, saying : "Why have you written that this man was the king of the Jews?"

2   Then the second of the men being crucified with Jesus spoke: "If you be Jesus Christ, save yourself, and save us from the great peril in which we find ourselves". The other condemned man answered, saying:

"You have no fear of God, and you are like the crowd yonder, for you have had a similar upbringing. It is fitting that we should be crucified, for we have committed much evil. Jesus, however, has not done the slightest wrong". He spoke then to Jesus: "O Lord", said he, "Remember me when you reach your own kingdom". Jesus answered him, saying: "I tell you truly that today you will be in my company in Paradise".

XI

1   It was the sixth hour of the day, and from that time, a great darkness came over the earth until the ninth hour. And the sun was obscured, and the dome of the temple split in two from top to bottom. The earth shifted and the land trembled greatly. Then Jesus cried out with a loud voice:" O Lord, I commend my spirit to your charge". Then he bowed his head, and his spirit departed from him.

2   A certain powerful man called Centurio, having seen these wonders, glorified God, saying: "That man yonder who was crucified and tortured is a righteous man". The people who were around him beat their breasts, and were greatly fearful and afraid. When Pilate heard these things, he became very sorrowful, and he called the Jews to him, saying: "Are you aware now of these great miracles performed for you?" The Jews replied: "These are no miracles, simply an eclipse which covered the sun in a manner which is normal".

3   The acquaintances of Jesus, and the women who had followed him from Galilee, were around the cross, grieving and lamenting at the sight of all that had been done to Jesus. Then there came forward a man who was good and righteous, truly pious and godly, charitable and judicious. He was called Joseph, and came from the city known as Arimathaea. He was a man who had no part in the sinfulness and iniquity of the Jews. He asked Pilate to allow him to take the body of Jesus from the cross in order to bury it, and Pilate granted him that permission. Then he removed the body of Jesus from the cross, bound it in the best white linen, and buried it in a place where nobody had ever been buried before.

XII

1 Now when the Jews heard that Joseph had asked for the body of Jesus, and had buried it, they sent a huge troop to look for him, and to look for the twelve men who had given testimony that Jesus was not born of a harlot. They were also seeking Nicodemus, and the others who had related the miracles and good works of Jesus. All of these had fled, and had concealed themselves except for Nicodemus alone. For he was a noble and powerful man amongst the Jews, and he said to them: "Why have you come into the church to pray after you have perpetrated the most momentous deed on earth, namely, the crucifixion and torture of Jesus Christ?" "Why, indeed, have you yourself come into the temple", they retorted, "since you sided with Christ, and may it be along with him that you find company in the afterlife?" "May it be as you say", said Nicodemus. There was another Jew who was being sought in like manner, who did not conceal himself, namely, Joseph. He said to the Jews: "Are you angry with me for having sought the body of Jesus from Pilate, and buried it, placing a stone at the entrance to the tomb? You did no good by crucifying that just man without cause. Indeed, not only did you crucify him, but you beat and stripped him, and pierced his side with a great spear". When the Jews heard this, they laid hold of Joseph, and they commanded that he be kept captive until after the Sabbath. They said to him: "We know that you do not deserve burial after being put to death, so we will leave your body to be eaten by the birds of the air, and the beasts of the earth". Thereupon Joseph said: "That speech is like the speech of the proud Goliath before David, on the day that they encountered each other. His pride was humbled, as will your pride, for God himself has said, through the mouth of his prophet, 'Leave vengeance to me, and I will exact it'. Pilate washed his hands in your presence, and swore by the sun and moon to you that he was innocent of the blood of the righteous man whom you crucified. And you answered him: 'Let his blood be upon us, and upon our descendants'. I fear that the anger of God will descend on you, and on your sons after you, and that he will utterly destroy you on account of the enormous deed which you perpetrated". When the Jews heard this speech, great anger and fury seized them. They took Joseph captive, and placed him in a closed chamber with no window at all. They put an iron lock on the door, and set two men to guard it, namely Annas and Caiaphas.

2	Then they took counsel with the priests and deacons of the people, and decided to gather in one place after the Sabbath, in order to resolve how to put Joseph to death. Now there assembled after the Sabbath the elders, priests, and leaders of the people, and they demanded that Annas and Caiaphas bring Joseph before them to be punished. They opened the door of the chamber, but found that Joseph was not there at all. It greatly astonished all the people that the door had been left closed, but that Joseph was not to be found inside the chamber.

XIII

1	As they were discussing this, they saw approaching them a band of the soldiers who were guarding the burial-place of Jesus. These called out: "Listen to us. As we were watching over Jesus's burial-place, a great darkness came over the sun, and the earth quaked and shook. Then we saw an angel of God by the stone which was at the entrance to the tomb. He was resplendent like the sun, and his garments as white as snow. In our terror of him, our strength and vigour deserted us. Indeed, we were like dead men. We heard the angel speaking with the women who were at the other side of the tomb, and saying to them: 'Do not be afraid, for I know that it is Jesus whom you seek, he who was crucified, and was buried here. He is no longer here, for he is risen from the dead, as he promised. Let you hurry to his apostles and disciples, and tell them to go to Galilee to meet him. He will have gone before you there, and you will see him then, as he foretold and promised you'.

2	The Jews were enraged and extremely angry with the soldiers in charge of the tomb, and they said : "Who were these women whom you saw, and what possessed you not to lay hold of them, and bring them with you?" The soldiers replied: "In our fear of the angel, we were like dead men. How could we take the women prisoner when we were in that condition?" The Jews answered them, saying: "We will pronounce the Lord alive only in his presence, for we do not believe anything of what you say". The soldiers responded, saying: "Why should you believe us? For he whom you saw raising the dead, curing every disease and illness, and performing all these godly miracles before you, that is Jesus Christ, son of the living God, not only did you not believe in him, but you crucified and tortured him for those very deeds of goodness. It is true, indeed", they said, "the Lord is alive, Jesus Christ, son of the living God, he whom you crucified and tortured. We have heard that you imprisoned Joseph for having entombed the body of Jesus, and that, after having left him in a closed chamber, when you opened it up, Joseph was not to be found therein. Let you, then, produce for us Joseph, the man whom you were guarding in a sealed chamber, and we will bring you the body of Jesus, which we were guarding in the tomb". The Jews replied: "We will bring you Joseph, so let you bring us Jesus. For Joseph is in his own city of Arimithaea". The guards answered back: "If, indeed, Joseph is there, so too is Jesus in the place called Galilee, as we heard the angel tell the women".

3   When the Jews heard this, they trembled with hate and fear and consternation. Amongst themselves they said: "If these tidings are heard publicly throughout the land, all of the people will believe in Jesus". They they gathered money, and gave it to the guards of the tomb, telling them to say that while they were asleep the body of Jesus was stolen from them. The guards took the money, and did as they were told by the Jews.

XIV

1   While these discussions were taking place, they saw approaching them a priest and deacon and teacher from Galilee, and in the church, in the midst of the temple, these said to them: "The Jesus whom you crucified we have seen, seated on the summit of Mount Olivet, in the company of eleven disciples. And he was saying to them: 'Go throughout the whole world, and preach about me to all the peoples, and proclaim my tidings. Baptize everyone who believes in you in the name of the Father, Son, and Holy Spirit. He who believes will be saved, and he who will not believe will be damned'. After he had said this, we saw him go up in the midst of the clouds to heaven".

2   When the chief priests and elders of the Jewish people heard this, they said to the three [who had given testimony]: "Give glory and honour to God, and affirm in our presence whether these things which you tell us are true". "We swear", they said, "by the God of Abraham, and the

God of Isaac, and the God of Jacob, that we saw Jesus, as we have related, and if we were to conceal what we saw, we would be commiting sin". Then the chief priest rose, and gave the three a large hoard of money in return for their concealment of their tidings. People were sent to escort them out of the land, lest they remain any longer among the people.

3   Then the Jews assembled in one place, and wrung their hands and made great lamentation, saying to one another: "What is this prodigious sign being manifested in the land of Israel?" Two Jewish leaders, the priests Annas and Caiaphas, rose to hearten the people, telling them not to be dejected or troubled. They said: "Do you wish to give credence to the guards of the tomb? For they are of foreign race, from outside this country, and they accepted payment from us in return for their concealing what we wish to be concealed. How do we know that that they did not take similar payment from the disciples of Jesus as a reward for saying that he had risen from the dead?"

XV

1   At that, there stood up an outstanding nobleman among the people, whose name was Nicodemus. "Beloved kinsmen", said he, "did you hear those three swear that they saw Jesus on the summit of Mount Olivet, among his apostles and disciples, and that they saw him afterwards ascend to heaven? Let you not wonder at that", said he, "for holy scripture relates that the prophet Elijah was borne to heaven in his earthly body. And when the people asked the prophet Elisha: 'Where was our father taken?', he answered that he had been brought to heaven. Therefore, we should go to look for Jesus to Mount Olivet, where he was seen, to discover if he is to be found there. And if we find him there, let us repent of our sins, and do him reverence".
        The Jews then selected a troop to go in search of Jesus. These set out, and spent three days traversing the mountains of Israel without finding Jesus. They returned, saying: "We did not find Jesus, but we found Joseph in the city called Arimathaea".

2   When the Jews heard that Joseph was in that city, they rejoiced greatly, and they made enquiry as to how they could bring Joseph to them to

relate his story. They took parchment, and wrote a letter on it, the words of which were: "Peace and joy to you, O father, Joseph, and to all who are with you. We acknowledge that we sinned, and that we betrayed Jesus, and you also. Though we acted thus, it would be right for you to come to speak with your fathers and children, and your own race. For it is a great wonder to us how you got out of the chamber in which you were detained. Grievous, indeed, was the plan which we proposed to carry out against you, yet God saved you from our hands, and from the malice of our decision. Peace, then, to you, O lord Joseph, and great honour from all of the people". These were the words of the letter to Joseph.

3   The Jews choose seven friends of Joseph, and sent them with the letter to Joseph, saying: "When you reach the place where Joseph is, give him this letter into his hand". The seven went to the place, and gave the letter into Joseph's hand, and when he read it he said: "Blessed is our Lord, the God of Israel, he who saved me from the hands of that people, so that they did not shed my blood". And Joseph kissed the messengers who came with the letter.

4   An ass was provided for him, and he mounted it, and travelled to where the Jews were. When the people heard this, they all came to meet him, and kissed him. Joseph said: "Peace, O Lord to all the people". Nicodemus took him to his own house that night.

5   And on the morrow the leaders of the people assembled there to question Joseph, saying: "Confess now to God, your Lord, and reveal truly to us all that we enquire of you. We were greatly angered and saddened by your burial of Jesus, and we imprisoned you in a chamber, and shut it fast. Then, when we opened it, we did not find you within. This astonished us very much. Tell us now what happened to you, and how you escaped".

6   Joseph replied, saying: "After you shut me in the chamber at evening-time, I was praying until midnight. And then I saw an angel at every corner of the house, and Jesus Christ in the centre. I am not able to describe his resplendence adequately. In fear, I threw myself face downward on the ground. He took my right hand in his, and raised me up, shook rose-water on me to clean my face, and kissed me. He said

to me: 'Do not be afraid, Joseph. Look at me, and recognize who I am'. I looked at him, and said: 'Greetings, Elijah', to Christ. He said: 'I am not Elijah. I am Jesus, in the body which you buried'. I said to him: 'If that be so, show me the grave in which in which I laid you'. He took my hand, and showed me the empty tomb where I had buried him, and the linen cloth which I had put around his body. It was then that I recognized that it was Jesus who was there. I did homage to him, and bowed down before him, saying: 'Blessed is he who has come in the name of the Lord'. He took my right hand again, and said to me: 'Peace be with you. Do not leave your own house for forty days. I am going to the place where my disciples are'. With that, he left me".

XVI

1   When the Jews heard the news related by Joseph they were profoundly startled, and fell on their faces as if dead.

2   They lamented among themselves, asking: "What is this sign which has been manifested in the land of Israel?" A certain deacon rose up from among the people, and said: "I knew the mother and father of Jesus, and some of his kindred. They always did reverence in the temple, and gave offerings to God. One day they came into the temple with the infant Jesus. There was a renowned old priest in the temple, whose name was Simeon. He took the child in his arms, and said : 'O Lord, take to yourself your own servant now, for now I have seen with my own eyes the saviour destined before all the peoples. He will be a light to succour the Gentiles, and a glory to the people of Israel'. Moreover, he blessed Mary, the mother of Jesus, and told her: 'I will reveal to you some of the tidings of that child. He was born to raise up many, and to cast down many. And a sword will pierce your soul, if you be his mother'. And I myself heard that conversation taking place", said the deacon.

3   The Jews then said: "Let us send people again to look for the three who said that they saw him on Mount Olivet".

4   The three were duly brought before them.

5   And on their arrival each of them in turn was called, and the same

questions were put to them, and they were unanimous in their answers, swearing by the law of God that they had seen Jesus, as they had reported.

6   Then Annas and Caiaphas said: "It is in our law that all evidence and testimony ought to be believed when it comes from two or three, and the three yonder have affirmed that they saw Jesus on Mount Olivet. What are we to do about it? These signs and affirmations which have been manifested among the people cause us great wonder. Enoch was conveyed by the word of God into paradise. We do not know what death took off Elijah. Then there is Jesus, handed over to Pilate, having been scourged, and a crown of thorns placed on his head, and his side pierced by a spear. He was crucified on a cross, and buried by the respected elder, Joseph. Now this same Joseph attests to us that he himself saw Jesus alive, after his death and burial".

THE DESCENSUS AD INFEROS

I(XVII)

1   Then Joseph stood up, and said: "Dear brothers, truly you should marvel at hearing that Jesus was seen, risen from the dead after he had gone to heaven. You should marvel, furthermore, that not only did he rise from the dead, but he also resurrected many others. These are still alive in Jerusalem, where they were definitely seen. Let you go now to look at their graves, and you will find them open. They themselves are now in the city of Arimathaea, praying constantly, speaking to no-one, and having the appearance of the dead. Let us go to them now and render them honour and great respect, and beseech them to relate to us tidings of the resurrection".

2   There were four there, Annas, Caiaphas, Nicodemus, and Gamaliel. They found the graves opened, with nothing therein. They went from thence to the city called Arimathaea, and found them there, genuflecting and praying, kneeling on the ground. They greeted and kissed them affectionately, and brought them with them to Jerusalem. They brought them into the temple, shut them in, and put the ancestral

scripture into their hands. They requested them by the God of Jerusalem, the God of Abraham, and of Jacob, and of Isaac, to tell the people how they themselves had risen from the dead, and what they had seen.

3   Then two of those who were resurrected, whose names were Carinus and Leuicius rose. They affirmed that they were two sons of Simeon, the just man whom we have mentioned earlier. They trembled, sighed, and raised their eyes to heaven. Then they made the sign of the cross with their fingers over their tongues, and they said: "Bring us parchment, so that we may write down all that we have seen and heard". This was brought to them, and they wrote thus:

II(XVIII)

1   O Jesus Christ, Lord and God, the resurrection of the dead and the life of the living, permit and allow us to speak of the signs accompanying your crucifixion, since we have been asked by your name to relate them to the people. For you yourself, O Lord, already ordered us, your servants, in our land to tell people of your divine glory. Therefore, beloved kinsfolk, listen to us as we relate tidings to you in our own way.

2   As we were in the company of our fathers and mothers in the depths of hell, a golden ray of sun suddenly illuminated the majestic great prison around us, so that we could all see each other clearly. Then our father Adam rose, along with all the patriarchs and prophets, and they rejoiced greatly. They said: "The light gives rise to the eternal light which our own everlasting luminary, the Heavenly Father, promised to send to our assistance".

3   Then Isaiah son of Amos, chief eminent prophet amongst the prophets, rose and said in a loud voice: "This light is the light of the son of the Heavenly Father, as I told you once upon a time when I was alive, proclaiming these words to you: "The people who are in darkness will see a great light, and those under the sway and shadow of death will have a great brightness shine on them". And you see that my prophecy has now come true. For now the everlasting light comes to us here in the gloom of death".

4   As we were discussing this, the noble ancestor Simeon rose and said: "Beloved people, glorify your lord, Jesus Christ, son of the living God, for once, when I was alive, I took him as an infant in my arms in the temple, and, prompted by the Holy Spirit, I said: "O Lord, accept my spirit, for now my eyes have seen your salvation, the salvation you have prepared for the whole people. He is a light and a glory to all the people of Israel" And that light which you now see is the light of Jesus Christ, son of the living God".

5   While Simeon was saying this, a man rose up, resplendent like a ray of sun. He was unknown to all, and the whole people asked him: "Who are you?" He answered them, saying: "I am John, the voice and prophet of Jesus Christ, son of the living God. My mother was pregnant with me while his mother was carrying my Lord. His mother was Mary, and my mother was Elizabeth. When Mary approached, while I was in my mother's womb I said: "This is the Lamb of God, who takes away the sin of the world". Later I baptized him with my own hands in the river Jordan, and after the baptism I saw the Holy Spirit descend in the form of a dove over his head, and I heard a voice from heaven saying: "This is my beloved son in whom I am well pleased". And I have come to you to tell you that he comes now to find you, to deliver you from the darkness in which you exist".

III(XIX)

Now, when John the Baptist had said this, the noble pre-eminent parent, our father Adam, rose and cried out in a loud voice: "Beloved son, Seth, tell your own sons and your family, that is, the patriarchs and prophets, what you heard from the Archangel Michael when I sent you to the gates of Paradise to ask God to send his own angel to me with the oil of the tree of mercy to anoint my body in my illness". Seth rose and answered: "Beloved father, I was praying at the gates of Paradise as you told me, when I saw Michael the Archangel approach me, and he said to me: "I was sent from my Lord to speak to you, Seth. Do not expend any more tears or prayers beseeching God for oil from the tree of mercy to anoint your father, for it cannot be had on this occasion, nor can anyone else receive that oil until the end of the time when five thousand and ninety-nine years years are completed".

"Then the beloved son of the Heavenly Father, Jesus Christ, son of the living God, will come, and will revive the body of Adam, along with the bodies of many others among the dead. He will baptize him in the river Jordan, and after the baptism he will himself bring the oil of the tree of mercy to all those who believe in him. He will grant eternal life to everyone baptized in his name, and in the name of the Holy Spirit, and he will bring your father, Adam, with him into Paradise, where the tree of mercy stands".

IV(XX)

1   When the patriarchs and prophets, and all the other holy people, heard this they rejoiced greatly. Then Satanus, the master and lord of death and Hell rose, and said to Hell and its officials: "Prepare yourself to accept the soul of Jesus, he who has been glorifying himself lately in the world as the son of God, though he was human, and in fear of death. For before his crucifixion, in my own presence, he said: "My soul is sorrowful facing death". Satan continued: "Great is the amount of harm done me by Jesus, and I order that he be punished for it. For there were many people whom I blinded, and others whom I made lame and bent, and more whom I made lepers in the world, and Jesus healed them all without fatigue or labour, simply with words. Moreover, there are souls of dead people whom I brought to you to torture, and he dragged them back to their own bodies, and revived them in turn".

2   Then Hell replied to Satan, the leader of the demons: "Who is this great powerful man who is fearful of death, despite having such powers? For every powerful one ever to come into the world is in my grasp, having been brought to me by you, through your own power. That being so, where has your power gone, since Jesus, who was fearful of death, is able to withstand death? I tell you truly, if he has that amount of power in his human form, so much the greater is his power in his divinity, and there is nobody able to withstand his might. He could take you by force, and could cause you woe forever". Satanus, lord of Hell, answered: "What doubt and fear seizes you about receiving this adversary into your grasp? For I attacked him on earth, inciting the mind of the Jewish people to anger and envy against him, and I thrust

a spear into his side and pierced it. I also mixed gall and vinegar, and gave him a drink of it, and I prepared a cross for him on which he was hung. He is still on the cross, and his death draws near. Once his spirit departs from him I will bring him to you to punish and torture him".

3 Hell replied, and said: "You told me, O Satan, that he is the one who dragged souls of the dead from my power and grasp. I have many people here whom he summoned. He is someone who, while alive in the world, released people from death, not by his own power, but by his prayers to heaven and to God. Jesus, then, without assistance or help, but by word alone, brought the dead out of my clutches. I was obliged to let out the soul of Lazarus, though his body had been decaying in the grave for three days and three nights, because of a single word of command. For when the soul of Lazarus heard Jesus say over his grave: "Arise, Lazarus", Lazarus bestirred himself, and leapt up in swift flight, and neither I nor my household were able to oppose him, so that he returned to his earthly body again". "When I heard the command of the word of Jesus, I was trembling and shaking with fear and terror before that voice. Now I understand that he who did that deed is almighty, and I beseech you, O ruler of Hell, by that great power which I know you to wield, that you will not allow the one who performed that deed to come to me to my dwelling. For if he should come, we would be reduced to subjection to him forever after, and all the people whom I have in bondage and captivity here, he will free them all, and will take them with him to divine life".

V(XXI)

1 While Hell and Satanus were thus conversing, they heard a voice like thunder or like a supernatural clamour at the entrance to Hell. It said: "Open your gates, and break the locks, so that the King of glory may enter". When Hell heard that voice, it cried out in a loud voice: "O Satanus, depart and leave my household to me, and if you be a powerful warrior, go and fight now against the King of glory, and do not allow him to defeat you, or to defeat us". At that, Hell thrust Satan out past the gates, and told his officials: "Shut your stout bronze gates, and strengthen them with iron locks, and keep a strongly-armed watch for the raider who is coming to bring you into subjection

forever".

2   The saints, and the noble prophet David, heard that conversation, and
     David rose and said: "I foretold these words to you at the time when
     I dwelt in the world: "He is the one against whom bronze doors and
     iron locks do not prevail, coming to assist the people who are in
     darkness". Then Isaiah son of Amos rose, and said : "I prophesied this
     when I was alive: "This is the young man who will be called Emman-
     uel... He will be able to defeat evil and exalt good, and the gates of Hell
     shall not prevail against him. After his resurrection, the dead in the
     graves will arise with him, once they taste of the drop which brings
     them salvation, namely, Jesus Christ".

3   When all the blessed ones heard that, they said to Hell: "Open your
     gates, for your power has been taken from you, and you have been
     vanquished". Then they heard the loud voice like thunder outside the
     entrance, saying: "Open your gates for the King of glory to enter".
     When Hell perceived that voice again at the gate, it said, as it did not
     know: "Whose is the voice seeking entrance?" The prophet David
     replied, saying: "I recognize the voice at the gate, for I prophesied
     about it by the grace of the Holy Spirit when I was alive, as I already
     told you. I declare now that it is the Lord and King of glory who is at
     the gate, the son of the Heavenly Father who came of his own accord
     from the heavenly dwelling in the form of his own servants, in
     humility and modesty, to listen to your mean speeches, your com-
     plaints and moans and illnesses, those of your own people, and those
     of us who are in your company, held in captivity by Satanus. There-
     fore, O depressing, foul, dark, dismal Hell, open up your gates so that
     the king of glory may enter". After David had said this, the gates
     opened on their own, the locks shattered, and the King of glory entered
     in human form and appearance.

                              VI(XXII)

1   The place which never before was lit became bright, and the bonds of
     inherent death, that is, of Hell, were broken. Hell was startled to see
     these signs, and was left without strength or power. When the officers
     of Hell saw that Jesus Christ was in their dwelling, and bright light to

and fro throughout Hell, something which they had never before experienced, they cried out, saying loudly: "Who are you, who has shown great offence to us, and to our powers? Who are you, who are so great and mighty, humble, and like an emperor, a fighting man and like a knight, wonderworking, and in the form of a servant, you who are King of glory over the living and the dead?" "It surprises us greatly that you should have been crucified, that you should die, and be buried, and that you now come alive to us. You had changed colour as all creatures do at death. Not only that, but the stars and constellations commingled, and the earth shook when you died. And now you are among the dead, and you are alive in our midst. You harassed our legions, and overcame our powers, so that we can scarcely talk to you. It is great audacity on your part that you are summoning, and taking with you to the place of ancestral freedom, those who are held in captivity and bondage by us, as a result of the original sin of Adam and Eve. Who are you, before whom our darkness retreated?. You shone the radiant eternal light on the blind who were our captives, so that they see each other, and see us, and see yourself besides". Then all the legions of demons grew fearful, and they cried out in a single wail, and with one voice: "Where have you come from, O strong resplendent Jesus, full of glory and brightness, without fault or sin? Alas for us to be like this, for until now the earthly world, from which you came to us, was under our domination. No dead person like you was ever brought to us before, for all the dead who came to us up to now were in terror of us, but we are in fear and apprehension of you. Therefore, who are you, you who have come intimidatingly, and without permission, to our territories and ancestral home?. You are not afraid of our torture or our punishment. Not only that, but you are seeking to bring our prisoners and captives with you to eternal glory. It appears that you are the one God of whom our leader, Satanus, spoke, saying that, through the outcome of the crucifixion, you would draw the power of all the world to yourself".

2   Then the King of glory suppressed death beneath his feet.

VII(XXIII)

1   He seized Satanus, the leader of Hell, bound him, and cast him down

to the depths of Hell. Thereafter Hell received Satanus, and proceeded to rebuke him greatly, saying to him: "O chief of destruction, lord of immoderation, foe of the angels, antagonist of truth and of the righteous, how did you allow, and how did you contemplate letting the King of glory be crucified? Why did you promise us his soul thereafter to torture, and much more besides?" "You lacked knowledge like one unlearned. Look how you fulfil what you promised. Do you see Jesus now, clearly having banished all the darkness of Hell by his own brightness? He broke all bonds, releasing all those who up to now were subject to us, in lamentation and groaning. These are now deriding us. Not only that, but the human race now no longer fears us. Rather, it is threatening us. Thus, O lord of all evil, deserter of eternal light, why has this happened through your agency? Why did you allow them to be given this cause for pride? See now those who from the beginning of the world to the present had no expectation of salvation or life, and no cry or sorrow or lamentation is heard from them now. Moreover, no trace of tear or sadness appears on their faces".

2   "O Satanus, O chief of destruction, and possessor of malediction, you were not long wasting the resources of Hell, the great store which you brought with you through the seizure of the tree of life in Paradise, when you urged the crucifixion without reason of Jesus Christ on the tree of the cross. Now your happiness has ended, and your sadness and grief has begun for eternity. Now you will understand how much torture and various pains you will suffer in my clutches from henceforth until Doomsday". Hell said furthermore to Satanus: "O instigator of death, fount of pride, you were entitled to ask for a cause or reason why Jesus deserved to be crucified, and when you found none, why did you allow him to be unrighteously crucified, without crime or justification for punishment? As a result of this, both we, and yourself have been sent astray forever".

3   After that speech of Hell to Satanus, Jesus Christ, King of glory, spoke to Hell: "I give you authority over the devils, Satan under your command and power forever, in place of Adam and his righteous descendants whom I will bring with me now to my own kingdom".

VIII(XXIV)

1   Then he stretched out his hand, and said: "Come to me, beloved holy
ones, who bear my own image and likeness. For you were condemned
because of a tree, and because of the devil. And you have been saved
because of a tree, and because of me". He took Adam by the right hand,
and said to him: "Peace to you, and to all your righteous descendants.
When I created you, I did not intend you to be in this dwelling. Come
with me now to my own kingdom, for you are of my body and my
blood". Then Adam bowed his head before the knee of his Lord, and
he gave liberal spontaneous thanks, saying in a loud voice, "I thank
you, O Lord, who has saved me from my enemies, my God and my
Lord, God of my salvation, God of my life. I cried out to you, and you
saved me, bringing my soul out of Hell, from the talons of the Devil.
You freed me from those who fell in the mire. Come ye holy and just
people, and render thanks to your God and Lord for liberating you
from the great captivity in which you languished". Then all the blessed
knelt down at the feet of the Lord, and said aloud: "O redeemer and
saviour of the world, what you promised through the law and the
prophets you have fulfilled. You have purchased life through your
crucifixion, and you have come because of your honour from a cross
of crucifixion to us to save us from the depths of Hell, and from death.
As you claimed your glory in heaven, you reached out with a cross on
earth. O Lord, place the sign of the cross on Adam, and on his
descendants".

2   Then he took Adam's hand, and brought him out of Hell, and all the
blessed followed. Thereupon David cried out with a loud voice: "O
holy and righteous people, sing out rousing music and harmony to
your Lord, with the choral song of archangels, to the one who performed great miracles for you, for his hand has saved you, o noble
faithful". All the blessed responded that they gave glory, honour, and
magnification to their Lord, as they said "*Alleluia, Alleluia, Alleluia*".

3   Then a holy prophet, Habakkuk, rose and said: "I thank you, O Lord,
for having come to save the people, and to free us from our darkness".
The prophet Isaiah rose then, and cried aloud: "O Lord, what king or
god is like you, who could do what you have done, to take away our
sins and our unrighteousness, and to save us from the grasp of the

Devil, as you once promised our forefathers in days of yore". All the blessed replied, saying: "He is our God and our Lord who will govern us forever". And all the prophets in turn cried out very loudly in this manner.

IX(XXV)

Then Jesus Christ placed Adam's hand in the hand of the Archangel Michael, and said to him: "Take Adam, with all his righteous descendants, to Paradise. I am going to assume my body, so that I may go in bodily form to heaven". Thereafter, the Archangel Michael, with the hosts of archangels, the saints, and the just, came to the gate of Paradise. They met there with two noble aged men, of patriarchal and saintly appearance. These gave a great welcome to the host which they saw arrive. Adam and his descendants asked them: "Who are you two, who have not been with us up to now, you who are bodily in Paradise?" The two responded, and one of them said: "I am Enoch, who, by the word of God my lord, has been brought here for as long as I live. Here with me is the prophet Elijah, who, by the words of the Lord, was brought here in a fiery chariot. We have not tasted death to the present day, nor will we, until Antichrist comes at the end of the world, when we have to go to Jerusalem to fight against him. We will kill him there, and three days afterwards we will be brought alive, in our bodies, to Paradise among the clouds of heaven".

X(XXVI)

While the host was there, they saw a certain dark, ugly image approach them with the sign of the holy cross on its shoulder-blades. The blessed looked at him, and asked: "Who is this, for as we look at him, his appearance appears to us to be that of robber? How is it that the sign of the holy cross is on his shoulders?" He answered and told them: "It is true that I am a thief, for every evil which I could have done on earth I did, and the Jews crucified me along with Jesus Christ. Then I saw the great miracle performed instantly on earth through his crucifixion. I believed that he was the creator of all the elements, the almighty High-King, and I beseeched him: "Remember me, O Lord, when you come to your kingdom". He accepted my prayer, and said to me: "I tell you truly, today you will be with me in Paradise". And after he had said this, his spirit departed from him, and my soul left me. He went to Hell to fetch you, and told me to go before him to Paradise. He put the sign of the cross on my shoulder-blades, saying to me: "Go to Paradise, and if the angel guarding Paradise will not let you in, show that sign of the cross to him, and say to him that it was Jesus Christ, son of the living God, who was crucified by the Jews, who sent you ahead of himself". "And when I said this to the angel guarding Paradise, he welcomed me warmly, and placed me in the midst of eternal life in Paradise. And he told me: "Wait awhile, and soon you will see your great forefather, Adam, approach you, with all his just descendants, to be in eternal life forever". When all the patriarchs, prophets, and holy ones heard those words of the thief, they called out joyfully in unison, and said: "Blessed be our almighty Lord, father of eternal light and of mercy, who bestowed this grace and clemency on his sinners, and brought them from the starvation of Hell to his resting places to consume the food of Paradise without cease, eternally. From him we receive glory and honour forever".

XI(XXVII)

"O beloved people", said Carinus and Leuicius (for these were the godly sanctified witnesses whom we heard), "We do not venture to tell you any more of the tidings of the King of heaven and earth, for Michael the archangel told us when we rose from the dead: "Go ahead to your kinsmen to Jerusalem, and proclaim to them the resurrection of our Lord Jesus Christ, son of the living God, he who has revived you, and many people besides, and saints also. Do not speak to anyone, and be like the dead, and remain dumb until the occasion when you will be permitted to tell the blessed story of the resurrection". "And thus we were, when we saw you approach, and you asked us to relate tidings of the resurrection to you. We prayed to God that he would permit us, and he did so, and we told you what you have heard up to the present. Now, the Archangel Michael has come to us to take us to be baptized in the river Jordan, and thereafter to place us in the company of many others of our kin who rose from the dead along with us, and to bring us into the presence of the risen Christ, in the beautiful, delightful place where we will be, in our own bodies, until Doomsday.

Then we will go, after the glorification of our bodies, into the presence of God for all eternity. Now, beloved people, peace, concord, love, brotherhood, and belief in the Trinity be among you forever". Thereafter, all those who were resurrected went with Michael to the river Jordan, and they have not appeared since.

20. TEXTS RELATING TO THE BELOVED DISCIPLE

20 A. EPISODES FROM THE LIFE OF JOHN, THE BELOVED DISCIPLE

1   "Help me, O Creator,
     O Christ, O mighty Lord,
     angelic God the Father,
     without beginning or inception,
     without end or termination,
     without weariness or contempt,
     without fatigue or misfortune,
     O divine radiance,
     O son of the Virgin Mary,
     I cry out clearly and constantly,
     assist me in this peril,
     answer me and help me".

2   Thereafter, he signed and blessed himself with the sign of the cross,
     and he drank what poison was in the beautiful golden cup, And when
     he had finished drinking he said: "I pray you, O God, almighty Father,
     assume into faith and belief those for whose sake I have drunk this".

3   The crowds began to observe him silently after he had consumed the
     poisoned drink, and when they saw no harm or hurt being done to
     him, they all cried out aloud with piercing sound, praising God the
     Creator, and saying: "There is no God but the God who is worshipped
     by John, the splendid apostle".

4   As for Aristodemus, he did not believe, and the people proceeded to
     reproach him on account of the noble outstanding apostle. And
     Aristodemus came to the place where John was, and said to him: "I am
     still doubtful and unsure. If I were to see dead people being revived in
     the name of your God, then all the uncertainty in my heart would
     depart". The people responded to this, saying: "Shut your mouth, and
     cease your speech to the consecrated apostle of Christ, or else you

yourself will be burned, along with your householding and dwellings".

5   When John heard this conversation he told the crowds to be silent until he himself should explain through the grace of the Holy Spirit and of divine teaching ... concerning healing, curing fully, as do good physicians in the case of galloping diseases which are not relieved without supreme skill in medical science. Then John replied to Aristodemus, giving him his beautiful shining tunic, and saying: "Take this, and put it over the bodies yonder, and say 'The apostle of Christ sent me to you with his own tunic, to say to you: " Arise from the dead, in order that all may understand that death and life are in my power, and in the power of the Lord whom I reverence and entreat, Jesus Christ, son of the living God" ' ". Aristodemus did this, and when he had placed John's tunic over the dead bodies before him, and had said over them the words told him by John, swiftly and speedily they rose from the dead, and went joyfully to where John was. They bowed down and prostrated themselves on the ground, and asked him to baptize them. Moreover, they related tidings of the time when they were dead, that is tidings of the bright city of heaven, and tidings of the many monsters and beasts of hell.

6   When Aristodemus heard those stories he hurried to where the mighty proconsul was, and said these words loudly and with nobility:

"Come, powerful consul,
Hurry joyfully with me
to the great heavenly apostle
that we may be baptized.
Let us foreswear zealously
gods and base demons.
Let us follow Christ lovingly.
Let us atone for our evil practices.
let us avoid worldly delusions.
Invoke, and again invoke
the heavenly dwelling and its bright reward
Come, consul"

"What are you saying concerning John now, O Aristodemus?", said the proconsul. "He is a god in a human body", said Aristodemus, "For the drink which he consumed would have killed worldly men who drank it. Were it not that the power of the true God protected him, he would have died. Moreover, in the case of the two whom the same drink killed, all I did was to place John's tunic over them, and they arose completely well, without any sign of death or distress on them. Let us go and seek his forgiveness for having often reviled, insulted, and shamed him, and barbarously discredited him".

7   Then the proconsul and Aristodemus came to the fair apostle, John. With their hosts and multitudes they cast themselves down on the ground before the apostle, and they asked forgiveness for their sins. He began to pray for them with faith and mercy. And he gave thanks to God that so many people had been called to God, and detached from the devil. He told them to spend a week meditating on the matter. This they did, and thereafter they returned to John, who baptized them all, women, boys, and children, princes, lords, and leaders, servants and attendants.

8   Then they hurried swiftly and joyfully to the base unholy temples wherein were their insubstantial unmerciful gods. And they smashed and broke the demonic images, the strange idols, and the great idolatrous representations, reducing them to dust. They built a beautiful lofty church in honour of the eloquent beloved John, where the mighty Lord was honoured and served, and divine worship has continued there to this present day. And archbishops, bishops, priests, and psalmists were appointed throughout the whole Church at that time.

9   On one occasion, John rose, washed his hands and face, chanted the psalms for the canonical hour, and entered the church for the sacrifice of Mass. A handsome elegantly-attired priest called [S]Eusisp rose, and placed about his neck a very beautiful amice, highly ornamented with golden thread. He put on his body a fine-textured tunic, and on his left wrist a beautiful gold-threaded maniple. He put on also a finely-embroidered embossed silk stole, and, over all, a well-made chasuble, bordered with golden crosses. He proceeded to celebrate Mass. John of the bright blue eyes was paying careful attention to the sacrifice, and he perceived from the beautiful divine host, and the

chalice embellished with golden crosses, which were being held by the priest Seusisp, that the latter had a hidden sin.

10   Thereupon John wept copiously and very sorrowfully, and he bowed down to the ground, saying: "O God who called us together, do not repudiate us. O God who healed our diseases and loved us, do not repudiate us. O God who offered himself for us, do not shun us once more. I beseech you now, O God and Creator, Prince and Lord, that you may cleanse the soul of that tonsured priest, Seusisp, from the darkness of evil thoughts, and from the oppression of great sin which is upon him. For he is as one who is ensnared by the devil's noose, so that he is unworthy to offer sacrifice or to serve the mighty Lord".

11   When the priest heard those holy consecrated words, he abandoned the sacrifice, fled from the temple, and began to bewail his sins before God the Father, the Creator. Then the eloquent John rose and called Birro the deacon, and said to him: "Go to the place where Seuisp the priest is, and tell him to come in". When he came, he cried aloud, lamenting his sins, and said in front of all: "I implore God steadfastly and fervently to wipe out my sins". And he knelt down before them, and said these words:

"Disciple of the Lord,
ever-angelic John,
a goodly, handsome-haired man,
with bright blue eyes,
red-cheeked and fair of face,
with gleaming teeth and dark brows,
red-lipped, white-throated,
skilful and dexterous,
with supple lithe fingers,
fair-sided, light-footed,
noble, slender, and serene,
distinguished, bright with holiness,
friend of Christians,
expeller of the dark devil,
God's fine disciple".

God heard the prayer of the priest and acted on his behalf. And John the noble evangelist took the offering once more, and they sang the office and Mass thereafter with lasting good favour.

12   Now there were very many pious nuns, widows, and such holy persons following John, spending their lives listening to the splendid sermons which he used to deliver to the people. And they had no livelihood or substance, prosperity or riches, save for whatever alms John received from the Christians. They complained constantly, and found fault often with John, because in their eyes, the amount of goods and alms which John got from the people was very ample and substantial, yet their share of it seemed meagre to them. They said: "What does he do with it, since we do not get it for food and clothing? He desires that he himself be rich , but that we should be poor".

13   John heard this, yet he did not react with an angry outburst or uncontrolled rage, but went on with calmness and composure, until one day he chanced to be on a great wide bridge, where patient asses were drawing home hay. John drew out a good handful of the hay, and said: "O God whom I trust and follow, turn all of this into gold without delay". And John said to his companions: "Count all the gold". This was done, and there was found to be a hundred smooth rods of beautiful burnished gold. John said: "Beloved children, take the gold to the smelters". They took it to the nearest craftsman, and it was put over fire to smelt and refine it. They said that they had never found finer gold. Then the gold was handed to John, who dropped it into the deep waters and swift-flowing stream beneath the bridge. Everyone was astonished at this. John said: "If I had wanted unlimited gold and riches, I would have received them from the Lord himself. But I freely prefer to be poor and lowly, for the kingdom of heaven belongs to the poor in spirit, as the Creator has said. And tell the hypocritical widows that the only thing I do with what I receive is to give it to them, and to other poor people. For the garment which I put on when I became an apostle of my Lord is none the worse yet, as far as its sheen and material and border is concerned, nor are the shoes any the worse, nor will they be, as long as I live. Moreover, Christ granted to us a knowledge of the seventy-two existing languages, so that we understand them as well as we do our mother-tongue".

14   One day as John was travelling, he saw approaching a fully-armed

soldier, ready to kill him. When he was in the presence of the apostle, the soldier said brutally and threateningly: "Very soon you will be under my control and power, and you will be killed with force by me". Thereupon John said: "May God extinguish your barbarous threat, your primed fury, and yourself also". With that, the soldier immediately left the spot and vanished, like smoke vanishes from a red-hot fire, or like dust disappears with the wind. For it was the devil who had come in the form of a soldier to do battle against John, on account of John's conversion to Christianity of many people who willingly served himself.

20B. FRAGMENT OF AN APOCALYPSE, AND DEATH OF JOHN

1   *(Beginning of text lost)*

2   "Then Christ sent the divine helper, the splendid holy angel Michael, to fight against arrogant Antichrist as he had fought against Lucifer. And Antichrist came in the form of a dragon to the summit of Mount Garganus to harm and attack the Christians. But Michael killed the dragon, and as a result, God and Michael were greatly glorified in heaven and on earth".

3   "This is the manner of Michael's appearance as he comes to fight Antichrist. He is radiant, fair of countenance, red-cheeked, with gentle steady long-lashed eyes, with eloquent red lips, and a white throat. He is shining with zeal, light-footed, angry, furious, aggressive, with his beautiful four wings spread around him, with a protecting sharp-edged splendid sharp ornamented slender sword firmly in his strong hand, to smite Antichrist in a manner befitting a noble angelic heavenly personage".

4   "With harshness, deep anger, bravery and strength, with swiftness and severity, strongly, fearlessly and terribly, he strikes Antichrist on the crown of the head, halving him on the spot in two splendid broad halves from the top of his head down to the ground. And that is the evil strange tale of Antichrist up to the present, as God confirmed to me", said John, the eloquent Beloved Disciple.

5   "The world will have three years of peace".

6   "And after all that, there will be a great silence throught the whole universe, so that neither the sound of the sea, nor the roar of the wave, nor the cry of the wind, nor bird-song, nor the sound of any created thing in the whole world will be heard for forty days and forty nights. Then the signs of Doomsday will appear, on the fifteen days before the Judgement".

7   "After these have come, four angels rise up from the four cardinal
     points of the world, and they call out loudly and impressively:'Arise!
     Arise! Arise! Arise!' ".

8   "Then the beautiful pure souls of heaven and the many evil souls from
     hell will go jointly with their bodies from the earthly graves in which
     they were buried to the judgement of Doomsday".

9   " And that is a brief account of the end of this bad world, as was nar-
     rated to me by the Creator, the good Lord", said John, the beloved
     apostle.

10   Thereafter John said to his disciples: "Go and make a burial-place for
     me in front of the altar. Cast out the earth far away from it, and make
     it very deep". This was done, and he himself went into it and lay
     readily down on the ground, and stretched up his two hands towards
     the Creator, saying:

11   "I thank you, O Creator,
     Christ, the mighty Lord,
     great Heavenly Father,
     gentle soft-spoken brother,
     excellent noble teacher,
     who gently and lovingly
     calls me to your banquet,
     who well understands
     that I desire to go
     to be with you in your kingdom.
     You perceive, O divine kinsman,
     how my heart has loved
     your truth and your word,
     loved to contemplate
     and look on you totally,
     I give you thanks".

12   "Thus am I", says John, "like one being revived from death, or being
     set free from imprisonment or from illness, in my delight at seeing
     your radiant countenance. For your appearance is fairer than every
     other, your words are sweeter than delicate honey-combs, and your

speech more eloquent than the speech of majestic angels. From early times I have prayed to you to bring me from this world to you, and you told me: 'Wait awhile, until you succour the people, and until they believe devoutly in me'. I thank you O heavenly Father, for you have saved my body from every defilement, and saved my soul from the seven sins, and you did not abandon me when I was being denounced and banished, and in every other difficulty besides".

13   "You granted that my lips uttered holy and true words in eloquent sermons, and you filled my body with the seven-fold Spirit, the Spirit of wisdom, understanding, fortitude, resolution, knowledge, love, and fear. And I assumed unto myself the seven virtues".

14   " I wrote all the gospel teachings concerning your wisdom and grace for your acquaintances and for your Church, and I looked after and protected your people up to the present time".

15   "Now I entrust and hand over your people believing in Christ, who have obtained wisdom, true knowledge, and sagacity, and have been blessed and baptized. Take me to you, as you promised me in the company of my brethren, Paul, Peter, Matthew, and Thomas, and the other apostles, so that I may partake of the the great feast which you created from the beginning, and which has no end. Open the divine gates and beautifully-draped windows, and the path which is undarkened by the devil, without opposition, without hostile onset. Send your splendid angelic messenger to cherish and protect [me], for you are the almighty Christ, Father, Son, and Holy Spirit, who lives and flourishes for all eternity". And all the people answered: "Amen".

16   Then a great brightness came upon the people for the space of one hour of the day. Such was the extent of the illumination that it could not be looked on. Everyone threw themselves on the ground. Then there came to them a beautiful fragrance, and perfume of angelic incense.

17   Thereafter they raised their heads, and looked at the burial-place. They found nothing there in place of the valiant priest, the eloquent judge, the devout helper, the wise preacher, the splendid confessor, the merciful dispenser of forgiveness, red-cheeked and blue-eyed, namely, John, the beloved apostle... And thus John parted from the

final things of this world.

18   The suffering and afflicted of the nearby district gathered to that place, and they were cured of all their ills.

19   As for the body of John, it is in a beautiful golden tomb, and at the end of each year, the best youth, who is without defilement or sin, is chosen, and he goes to cut John's hair and pare his nails, and when he has completed that task, he partakes of the body and sacrifice of Christ, and he himself ascends to heaven on that day.

Thus John's body remains without putrefaction or corruption. Indeed, it is as if it were in a deep sleep, and it will be thus until Doomsday.

21. THE ACTS OF PETER AND PAUL

1   After Paul reached Rome the Jews came to him and addressed him thus: "Protect and proclaim the faith in which you were born, for it is not fitting that you, a Jew, should undermine the Jewish faith. When you see Peter, oppose him. It is he who has subverted our teaching, in matters such as the sabbath, new moon, and circumcision". Paul said: "Go and tell Peter that we should meet, and if he preaches new doctrine I will confute him in your presence. However, if what he teaches has been confirmed by testimonies from the books of the Hebrews, we should submit to it, and give it our consent". When Paul had uttered these and other such statements, the Jews came to Peter, and said to him: "Paul has come from the Jews, and asks you to come to him. For they brought him hither as a prisoner, and will not allow him to go where he wishes until he comes before Caesar".

2   When Peter heard this he was much gladdened, and he came to him without delay. When they saw each other they wept with joy, and shed copious tears, each with his arm around the other's neck. Then Paul told Peter all that he had endured in coming, while Peter related to him all that he had suffered at the hands of Simon Magus. Peter departed at the close of the day, and when the morrow dawned he came back, and he found a large crowd before him at the door of the house where Paul was.

3   At that time there was great contention and disturbance between Jews and Gentiles, for the Jews proclaimed: "We are a chosen race, a royal kindred of the seed of Abraham, Isaac, Jacob, and all the prophets, to whom the Lord spoke face to face, and revealed his great miracles and secret mysteries. You, Gentiles, have nothing substantial or good in your heritage, only defilement from worship of stones and trees and idols". To these, and many other remarks, the Gentiles replied: "We, on hearing the truth, abandoned error and pursued righteousness. You, however, knew the God who was to be adored, you saw the

99

wonders and miracles of the prophets, you were given the Law by God, you crossed the Red Sea dryshod, you saw your enemies drowned before you, you were given manna from heaven, for you there appeared a column of cloud in the day and a fiery column at night, for you pleasant water flowed from a rock. Yet, after all these things, you constructed the golden calf and adored it. We, however, though we did not see those marvels and miracles, nevertheless we believed in the true God. You let him go from you without believing in him".

4   While they were engaged in this contention Peter and Paul preached to them and made peace between them. However, the Jewish leaders and the heathen priests stirred them up, and aroused the murmuring of the populace against the apostles. They praised Simon Magus in the presence of Nero Caesar. Moreover, they denounced Peter and Paul because innumerable people had turned to the Lord as a result of the preaching of the apostles. It was such, indeed, that Libia, wife of Nero, and Agrippina, wife of Agrippa the prefect, had converted to faith and belief, and left their royal palaces to render service to the Lord and to Christianity.

5   When Simon Magus observed the murmuring of the people against the apostles he proceeded to revile Peter, saying: "Peter is a magician and a false prophet". Those who marvelled at the wonders which he used to perform put their trust in Simon, for he induced movement in the bronze serpent, and impelled images of stone and brass to stir and be mobile. Moreover, he made himself appear to be flying through the air. Peter, however, for his part, was healing the sick and the blind and the lame, banishing demons, and resurrecting the dead. He admonished the people that they should shun the false teaching of Simon Magus. The Christians then proclaimed Simon to be a wicked sinful magician, while those who believed in Simon affirmed that Peter was a sorcerer.

6   When Nero heard these tidings he ordered that Simon be brought to him. On arrival, Simon transformed himself into various forms, the form of a youth, of an old man, yet another time, of a soldier. In such a fashion, through the assistance of the devil, he assumed many shapes. When Nero thus saw Simon he supposed him to be truly the

son of God. However, Peter proclaimed him to be a lying wicked magician. Then Simon said to Nero: "Listen to me, O ruler, for I am the son of God who has come from heaven. Hitherto I have endured Peter on his own. Now I am faced with doubly great trouble, in the person of Paul, who is fighting against me alongside Peter. You do not see that unless you plan the downfall of these men they will destroy your kingdom".

7   Nero said: "God teaches and loves everyone, yet you are the persecutor of these people". Simon Magus replied: "These people have converted all the Jews so that they no longer believe in me". Nero said to Peter: "Why do you not believe as do your people?" Peter said to Simon: "You could deceive all, but you were not able to deceive me, and God has enjoined on me the conversion of the error of all those whom you have led astray. I am amazed at your brazen impudence in the presence of the king in seeking to overcome the disciple of Christ by your sorcery, for you attempted this often before, but did not succeed". Simon said to Nero: "It is no less amazing to me, O ruler, that this ignorant person, Peter, is of any consequence to you. He is a lying fisherman, without merit as regards speech, family, or power. I will now order my angels to come and punish him". Peter said: "I do not fear your angels. Rather, they are more fearful of me, because of the strength of my God, Jesus Christ".

8   Nero responded: "Are you not afraid, Peter, of this man Simon who affirms his divinity with many wonders?" Peter replied: "There is no divinity in him at all, but he has two natures, human nature and diabolic nature". Moreover, Peter declared to Nero: "Let Simon, if he comes from God, proclaim what I am thinking, for God knows people's thoughts. I will tell you privately what I am thinking, O Nero. Ask that a barley loaf be brought hither to me in secret". This was brought, and he broke it, and put it into his sleeves. Peter said to Simon: "Let you tell what I have been thinking or what I have done, O Simon". "Do you think, Peter", said Nero, "that I would believe that Simon would not know that? For he has performed great wonders in my presence, and everything which he promised to do, he accomplished". Peter said: "If he has done great things, why does he not do what is small?" Nero said: "What answer do you make to that, Simon?" Simon replied: "Let Peter reveal what I am thinking". "It will now be manifest

that I understand Simon's thoughts", said Peter.

9   Then Simon grew angry, for he had not perceived what the apostle had
     been thinking, and he said: "Let large hounds descend and devour
     Peter in the presence of Nero Caesar". Suddenly hounds of startling
     size came and made to attack Peter. Peter, however, stretched out his
     hands in prayer, revealing to the hounds the loaf which he had blessed.
     When the hounds saw this they immediately turned back. Thereupon
     Peter said to Nero: "I told you that I knew what Simon was thinking,
     namely, that he would bring doglike angels against me, which were
     not angels of God". Nero said to Simon: "I think, Simon, that you have
     been vanquished". Simon replied: "He did this to me in the land of
     Juda and Palestine, and because he often contended against me, he
     learned these deeds from me".

10   Nero said: "You have been incited by envy against these people, for,
     as I see it, you are greatly jealous of their Christ. I fear, however, that
     you have been defeated and destroyed by them". Simon replied: "Do
     not be deceived, O ruler", said he. Nero answered: "I have not been
     deceived , but I see that you are an opponent of Peter and Paul, and of
     their master, Jesus". Simon said: "Christ is not the master of Paul at
     all". Paul retorted: "He who was physically present to teach Peter, that
     same man has instructed me through revelation".

11   Simon said to Nero: "I am surprised that you should should be in
     doubt about me, for I have performed numerous wonders and mir-
     acles before you". Nero replied: "I am not in doubt, and I do not believe
     in either of you. Simply give me an answer to what I am asking you".
     Simon said: "I will not answer you at all". Nero responded: "What else
     then for me but to regard you as of no account, for you are deceitful in
     all things, as I perceive from your deeds. The three of you have made
     me perplexed, so that I now do not know which God to accept". Peter
     said: "Believe in the Father, Son, and Holy Spirit, the creator of all the
     elements, who made heaven and earth, and all that is in them. He is the
     true King, whose rule is unlimited". Simon said: "Do you both not
     understand that you will get what you seek, that is, martyrdom?"
     Peter and Paul replied: "O Simon, O wicked magician, vessel full of
     demons and of bitterness, no good awaits you in this world or in the
     next".

12   Simon retorted: "Listen, O Nero, so that you may find out that these
      men are deceivers, while I assuredly come from heaven. I will go to
      heaven tomorrow. Then I will grant good fortune to those who believe
      in me, and I will reveal my anger and rage to those who reject
      me".Then Peter and Paul said: "God has called us long since to heaven,
      and to his great glory and honour. You, however, are called by the
      devil, and are hastening to eternal torture and pain". Said Simon: "O
      Nero, cast these madmen away from you, and let me be of benefit to
      you when I reach my father in heaven". Nero replied: "How are we to
      prove that you will go to heaven?" Simon said: "Order a large wooden
      tower to be made, and I will enter it. My angels will bear me from
      thence up in the air, for they cannot come down to earth to mingle with
      sinners".

13   Nero then ordered a high tower to be constructed on the Campus
      Martius, and he asked all the people, their leaders, and the apostles to
      come to witness the happening on the morrow. Nero said to the
      apostles: "It will soon be evident who is in possession of the truth".
      Peter and Paul replied: "It will not be revealed by us that Simon is a
      deceiver, but by our Lord, Jesus Christ". Paul turned to Peter, and said
      to him: "My part is to kneel and pray to the Lord, yours is to cast down
      Simon as he rises up, for you were first to be chosen by God". Peter said
      to Simon: "Make your attempt, for exposure of your iniquity will soon
      be upon you. The time draws near when we will invoke God, for I see
      my Lord Jesus Christ summoning me, and summoning Paul". Nero
      asked: "Which way will you go against my will?" Peter replied:
      "Whichever way the Lord Jesus Christ directs". "Is it to heaven you
      will go?", asked Nero. Peter answered: "We will go wherever is willed
      by the God who calls us".

14   Then Simon ascended into the tower in the presence of all, and
      stretched out his hands, and was flying in the air. Nero declared: "This
      man Simon is truthful. You and Paul, however, are deceivers". Peter
      said to him: "You will realise without delay that it is we who are truth-
      tellers and disciples of Christ, and that Simon is no god, but a wicked
      cheating magician". Nero said: "You still persist in your evil while you
      see him clearly going to heaven". Peter said to Paul: "Raise your head
      and see Simon flying". Then Paul responded: "O Peter, carry into
      effect that which you have set out to do, for our Lord Jesus Christ is

summoning us". When Nero heard their conversation he derided them, saying: "It is clear to these now that they are defeated, and that they are deranged". Peter said: "I request you, O servants of the devil, who have raised this man up in the air to lead the hearts of unbelievers astray, for the sake of the Creator of all things, for the sake of Christ who arose from the dead on the third day, let you not bear him up from this moment forward!". Immediately Simon fell down in the place called *sacra via*, and his body was broken in four parts. Four stones were formed there in commemoration of the triumph of the apostles, and remain to this day.

15   Thereupon Nero ordered the apostles to be imprisoned, and the body of Simon to be watched over for three days, for he thought that Simon would rise on the third day. Peter said to him: "He will never rise, for he has died to suffer pain and torment". Then Nero said to the prefect Agrippa: "These impious men are prisoners. Bring fiery swords to bear on them to put an end thereby to their lives, and the lives of all who side with them". The prefect replied: "O king and ruler, it is not fitting that their deaths should be similar, for Paul is not a convicted criminal, while Peter is a murderer and a reprobate. It seems to me that the just course is to behead Paul, but to crucify Peter". "You have given a satisfactory judgement", said Nero. Then the apostles were brought before Nero.

16   When Paul was taken to the place of decapitation he saw a certain woman with white linen cloth in her hand. Paul said to her: "Give me the linen cloth to put around my head, so that I may not see the hand of the executioner.You shall have it back immediately". The woman gave him the cloth. Paul was beheaded at the marble columns in the *via ostensi*, and the linen cloth came back again to the woman. Paul's head, however, immediately rolled away into a certain lake where it remained for forty years. After the fortieth year the daughter of the woman who had given the linen cloth to Paul came to wash clothes at the same lake. She saw lights shining in the lake, and made this known throughout the city. Then the Roman populace came hither, and found Paul's head in the middle of the lake. They bore the head in honour, with much hymn-singing, to where the body was. And both body and head were dripping blood, as though Paul had been beheaded on that very day. They settled the head on the body, and the two fused

together as though in life. Everyone praised and blessed the Lord on account of that miracle.

17   As for Peter, when he came to be crucified he said: "My Lord Jesus Christ who came down from heaven was crucified with his head upward and his feet downward. For my part, I am not worthy to be placed thus, so let my head be downward, and my feet upward". The executioners did so. Then an innumerable host gathered there, intent on burning Nero Caesar. But Peter called out, saying: "I came hence today to speak to a brother of mine, and my Lord Jesus Christ met me on the way. I adored him, and said to him: '*Domine quo vadis?*' 'Where are you going, Lord?' '*Et dixit Christus, uado in Roma crucifigi iterum*' 'And Christ said to me: "Follow me, for I am going to Rome to be crucified again', that is, to be crucified in the person of his followers, the apostles. Do not, therefore, hinder my passage", said Peter, "for I am going to heaven, since Paul and I are followers of Christ". When Peter had spoken these and other words, he yielded up his spirit.

18   Then holy persons appeared - angels, in fact, the like of whom was never seen before or since. These said: "For Peter's sake we have come from Jerusalem" (Jerusalem being the name used then for heaven). Thereafter they secretly took away Peter's body, and left it in the place named *Vaticanus*, saying to the Roman people: "Be glad and rejoice that these holy men and great anchorites are among you". Now the Romans conceived a great hatred for Nero, such that they determined to scourge and beat him to death. When Nero heard that plan, he was seized with intense fear and terror. He made a secret escape to the deserts and woods of the land, where he remained, wandering and astray, until he died of cold and hunger, and animals and birds devoured him thereafter.

22. THE PASSION OF THE APOSTLE PHILIP

1   The apostle Philip was preaching and teaching for forty years in Scythia. Heathens then came to him, took him prisoner, and brought him with them to the temple of Mars, who was their idol god. There was a huge dragon there, which had killed the two tribunes who were placed over the city by the Romans to levy the tribute of Caesar. And it was the impious keepers of that dragon who had imprisoned Philip. An enormous number of people in that city were suffering from various diseases as a result of the venomous emissions from that dragon. Some were made blind, others deaf or lame. And he brought upon them every other ailment also, so that they might offer sacrifices to the devil to cure those maladies, and thus their souls might be damned thereafter.

2   The apostle Philip said to all the people in the city who were ill : "Do what I advise, and you will be healed in body and soul. In the name of the Lord Jesus Christ, the demonic dragon who has formerly done you harm will be hunted out , and I will revive in the name of Christ those who were killed by it". The people said: "Just tell us what we are to do". "Cast out the figure of Mars, and break it", said Philip. "In its place put the cross of Christ, and then do reverence to that". "Simply grant us health", said they, "and we will then break the image of the idol Mars".

3   As a great silence fell, the apostle said: "Depart, dragon. Leave your lair in the name of the Lord Jesus Christ, and go to some place where humans do not dwell, so that you may never again do injury to anyone". Thereafter, at the word of the apostle, the dragon, surrounded by attendant demons, departed with a loud cry, filling the temple with its fumes and stench. And he did not appear again. Philip resuscitated the son of the priest who used to set fire to the sacrifices, and he immediately cured all the people who were made ill by the venom of the beast. Those who were formerly at variance with Philip converted to zealous repentance when they saw that great miracle.

They used to venerate Philip as if he were a god.

4   He preached there for a year, his instruction dealing with the manner in which Christ was born of the virgin, how he was crucified, how he ascended to heaven before the eyes of his apostles, and how the grace of the Holy Spirit came upon his apostles and gave them the gift of many tongues, though until then they spoke but the one language, Hebrew. "I am one of these apostles", said Philip. "I have been sent to reveal these things to you, that the idols which you worship are not true gods, but mute images, without intelligence or reason, the useless work of sinners' hands. Those who do them worship are truly the enemies of God". Multitudes then believed in Philip. There was no fewer than many thousands of people, who were all baptized by him. And numerous churches were built by him there, and he ordained bishops, priests, and deacons.

5   Then it was revealed to Philip in a vision that he should leave those lands and cities, and go to the bishop of Asia, to show him compassion, and to speak with him afterwards. The apostle Philip thus set out for Asia, and stayed in the city of Hierapolis, where he condemned and subverted the religion of the Ebonites, who held that Christ was not born of a virgin. Philip disparaged and banished that belief. Now Philip had two daughters, two excellent virgins, through whom God granted that innumerable other virgins were brought to faith and conversion.

6   Twelve days before he was crucified, Philip called to him all the priests, deacons, and bishops of the nearby cities, and said to them: "Only twelve days remain of my life. Let you be mindful of the teaching of the Lord Jesus Christ, and pray well to the Lord. Do battle bravely against your vices and sins. Show contempt and scorn for the ancient enemy, the devil, and his temptations. Subdue and restrain your bodily desires by fasting, prayer, abstinence, and giving food and clothing as alms to the poor and needy of the living God. God will fulfil his promises to us if we do all of these things. He will grant us peace and happiness in this life, and the kingdom of heaven for our souls after death. Indeed, God will increase his wonder-working in the churches on earth, for this has been the Lord's prophecy and promise to us, if we carry out these things to the best of our ability".

7   Then impious crowds, along with the Jewish priests, rose up against
     Philip, and said that his tongue should be cut out. This was done, yet
     it did not at all diminish his teaching of the people. The people and
     priests asked that his tongue be cut out again, but though it was done,
     it did not harm him. Seven times the apostle's tongue was cut out by
     them, yet he did not cease from preaching during that time. Then they
     asked that he be stoned. They struck him on the face with fists, lead
     cudgels, and stones, but they caused him neither injury nor any kind
     of pain.

8   Thereupon the people and priests ordered that the apostle should be
     crucified, since they failed to inflict any other death on him. A certain
     wicked cruel man among them came forward, and placed a deadly
     noose around the apostle's neck, and they hanged him then, after he
     had endured much pain, insult, and scourging, like his master, Jesus.
     Hierapolis, then, is the name of the city in which Philip the apostle was
     crucified. Great splendour and ministering angels were seen around
     the gallows when Philip expired, and the angels placed the soul of the
     apostle in the mansions of the kingdom of heaven in the glory of the
     angels, after his attainment of the crown of martyrdom.

9   The holy apostle Philip was eighty-six years old when he departed to
     the Lord. They buried his body in the village called Bethsaida. His two
     daughters, the two holy virgins, were buried there a long time later,
     one of them at the right side of the apostle, the other at his left. At that
     place, everyone who prays fervently to the apostle and the two holy
     virgins will have his request granted.

23. THE EVERNEW TONGUE

1   *In principio fecit Deus caelum et terram, et reliqua.* The High-King of the world, stronger than any king, higher than any power, fiercer than any dragon, gentler than any child, brighter than suns, holier than any ancient, more vengeful than all men, more affectionate than any mother, the only son of God the Father, he it was who gave this account of the formation and creation of the world to the many peoples on earth, because it was not known to anyone except God what any visible thing in the world was like, for it was as if the race of Adam had its head in a bag, or existed in a dark dwelling. For this reason, then, that there was no knowledge of the form of the world, or of who made it, this account came from heaven to open the mind and intellect of all, so that souls might find the way of life and salvation.

2   Now everything was obscure to the eyes of Adam's race except for their seeing the motion of the constellations, the moon, sun, and stars, which circulated each day without ever ceasing. They saw, moreover, that the springs and rivers of the world never stopped flowing at any time. They observed the depression on the earth, the debility and sleep afflicting light and crops at the coming of winter. They saw also the revival of the earth with heat and light, flowers and fruit, at the reawakening of summer.

3   Yet they did not know who was responsible for this until there came, as God arranged, the account of the creation of the world, its forms and motion. All of this was obscure until the story was related, until the Evernew Tongue revealed it, speaking from the height of heaven above the assembly of Mount Sion. For the hosts of the eastern world were gathered, those from the mountains of Abian as far as the shores of the Red Sea, and from the Dead Sea as far as the island of Sabarn. This was the number congregated, three thousand four hundred and eighty-five bishops, and fifty-four thousand nine hundred and sixty-nine kings of the world.

4   That assembly lasted for a year and four months, summer, winter, spring, and autumn, under nine hundred white linen awnings decorated with golden insignia, on the summit of Mount Sion. There were five thousand nine hundred and fifty pillared lights and precious stones which lit up to illuminate the gathering, in such a way that no bad weather could hinder it at any time. There were two hundred and fifty bishops, five hundred priests, three thousand in ecclesiastical orders, one hundred and fifty sinless youths, and five hundred high-kings with their retinues there before them. At midnight their voices would reach Jerusalem, as at each nocturns they came to sing the greetings sung in the holy heavens, *Gloria in excelsis Deo, et reliqua.*

5   Then the hosts of the assembly would come up between two plains , as the moving hosts and concourse returned to Mount Sion, with the music of their joyful greeting mingling with angelic music from the just ranks of the High-King.

6   Thereafter, suddenly, at the end of the eve of Easter, there was heard in the clouds a noise like thunder, or like the crackle of fire. There was a thunderous blast meanwhile, whereby suddenly a solar mass, like a bright sun, was seen in the midst of the tumult. That radiant solar mass revolved around in such a way that eyes could not look on it, for it was seven times brighter than the sun.

7   Immediately afterwards, as the eyes of the host awaited the crash, for they thought that it was a sign of Doomsday, there was heard a clear voice which spoke in angelic language *"Haeli habia felebe fae niteia temnibisse salis sal"*, that is, "Hear this account, sons of men. I have been sent from God to speak to you".

8   Then sudden weakness and fear came upon the crowds, and their fright was not unfounded. The sound of the voice came forth like the shout of a crowd, yet at the same time it was clearer and plainer than human voices. It resounded over the encampment like the call of a mighty wind, yet did not appear louder to each individual than the voice of a friend in the ear, and it was more melodious than music.

9   The Hebrew wise men responded, and said "Let us know your name, your status, and your message". The Evernew Tongue was heard,

speaking in an angelic voice: "*Nathire uimbae o lebiae ua un nimbisse tiron tibia am biase sau fimblia febe ab le febia fuan*", that is, "I was born among the peoples of earth, conceived by procreation of man and woman. My name is Philip the Apostle. The Lord sent me to preach to heathen peoples. Nine times my tongue was cut out of my head by heathens, and nine times I was able to go on preaching again. For this reason I am called the Evernew Tongue by the company of heaven".

10   The Hebrew savants said: "Let us know what language you speak to us". He replied: "I speak to you in the speech of angels, and of all the heavenly orders. Even the creatures of the sea, beasts, quadrupeds, birds, serpents, and demons know it. It is the language which all will speak at Judgement".

11   "It is this which has made me come to you, to elucidate to you the wonderful story which the Holy Spirit related through Moses son of Amram concerning the creation of earth and heaven and all visible thereon. For the narrative tells of the making of heaven and earth. Likewise, it concerns the creation of the world brought about by the resurrection of Christ from the dead on this Easter eve. For every substance, every element, and every essence visible in the world were all bound together in the body in which Christ arose, that is, in the body of every human".

12   "In the first place, there is material from wind and air. From it comes the capacity to breathe in human bodies. Then there is heat and burning fiery matter. This forms the red heat of blood in bodies. There is material from the sun, and from the stars of heaven besides. This makes the lustre and light in people's eyes. There is material made of bitter and salty elements, which forms the bitterness of tears, the gall of the liver, and much anger in human hearts. There is, moreover, material from stones and the clay of the earth, which causes the fusion of flesh and bones and limbs in people. There is material from flowers and coloured things of the earth, which engenders the variegation and paleness of faces, and the colour in cheeks".

13   "All the world rose with him because the essence of all the elements was in the body which Jesus assumed. For if the Lord had not been crucified on behalf of the race of Adam, and if he had not arisen after

death, the whole world and the descendants of Adam would be destroyed when Doomsday came. No creature of sea or earth would be regenerated, but the skies would blaze as far as the third heaven. All but three heavens of the great Heavenly Kingdom would remain unburnt. There would be neither land nor people, alive or dead, in the world, only hell and heaven, if the Lord had not come to redeem them. All would thus perish without restoration".

14 "For this I have come to you", said Philip, "to give you the information, for the formation of the shape of the world, as has been related from of old, is dim and obscure to you". "Well then", said the Hebrew sages, "tell us about the innumerable marvels which happened then, for the matter is eclipsed from us unless we have it clearly set forth".

15 The Evernew Tongue was heard speaking in angelic language:"*Lae uide fodea tabo abelia albe fab*", *quod latine dicitur: "in principio fecit Deus caelum et terram"*, and he said: "*Ambile bane bea fabne fa libera salese inbila tibon ale siboma fuan*". It would be tedious to recount in Hebrew all that was related there: that there was no order nor brightness, no earth with mountains and territories, no sea with islands, no hell with tortures before it was said "Let there be elements". The circuits of the seven heavens did not exist, nor clouds to water the earth, nor sparks, nor outbreaks of bad weather. There were no lands on which it might pour, for there was neither rain nor snow. There was no lightning, nor blast of wind, nor thunder. The course of the sun did not exist, nor the alternations of the moon, nor the variegation of the stars. There were no sea-monsters, nor sea in which they would swim. There were no streams, herds, beasts, birds, dragons or serpents".

16 *Responderunt sapientes Ebreorum:* "We ask what existed at that time when none of the things mentioned up to now existed?" The Evernew Tongue answered: "The marvel of all elements existed, that is, God, who is without beginning or end, without sorrow, age or decay. There was not a time or occcasion or era when he did not exist. He is neither younger nor older than at first. Nothing was impossible for him to do. He reflected, and had a thought. This thought had no beginning. He contemplated the existence of a more splendid thing whereby his power and his unutterable dignity might be seen, for these did not exist in any other things apart from himself".

17   "Finally, with these thoughts, he immediately created light. The light which he created was the circuit of the heavens with the nine orders of angels. There were seventy lands with six hundred and twenty four sunny dwellings, with melodies and colours in the seven forms of heaven. In a single day he made the circuit of those forms, giving the basis in which the world was made, for it is in the shape of a round circle that God first fashioned the world".

18   Then the Hebrew sages said: "Tell us now the manner of arrangements in the world, for we are uninformed and ignorant of any of them".

19   The Evernew Tongue answered: "Though you do not see it, every element happens to be round, in accordance with the shapes of the world. For the heavens were rounded, as were the seven seas surrounding them, and thus also the earth was made. And in circular motion the stars encircle the round wheel of the earth. It is as circular shapes that souls appear after going forth from bodies. It is as a circle that the circuit of majestic heaven is seen, and the circuit of sun and moon is rounded. All of this is fitting, for the Lord is as a circle, without beginning or end, he who always was, and always will be, he who created all of this. That is the reason why the world was formed as a round shape".

20   *Dixit pleps Ebreica:* "A question: What was in the round multiform circuit which was the basis of the world?"

21   The Evernew Tongue replied: "In the orbital circuit forming the matter of the world were cold and heat, light and dark, heaviness and lightness, wet and dry, high and low, bitter and mild, strong and weak, the roar of the sea and the sound of thunder, the scent of flowers, the chant of angels, and pillars of fire".

22   "All of these were in the round multiform mass which was formed from the matter of the universe", said he. "There the makings of hell were generated also, for hell was not created in the first place until the archangel transgressed and evaded the law of the King who had created him along with the innumerable host of angels. Up to then hell was not created", he said, "but the material for it existed in genesis in the circular multiform mass out of which was fashioned the earth, and

all the races of the world. And if the angels who sinned had maintained the nature in which they were created, and their angelic brightness, the material of hell would have been converted into a beautiful brilliant kingdom, like the kingdom of the holy angels".

23 This, then, is the work of the first day on which God began the creation of the world, *licet scriptum est: Qui uiuit in aeternum creauit omnia simul.*

24 *Artibilon alma sea sabne e belioa flules elbiae limbae lasfania lire: quod latine dicitur: Fecit quoque Deus firmamentum inter aquas et diuisit aquas quae erant super firmamentum ab his quae erant sub firmamento.*

25 On the second day God made the surrounding vault of the seven heavens, and the heavenly waters. For the Lord knew at the time he created the world that Man would transgress the precept given him. Thus a screen for heaven was placed so that men should not face directly or look at the beatitude of heaven and the throne of God.

26 *Interrogauerunt plebes Ebreorum: "Indica nobis naturas absconditas et misteria septem caelorum et quinque zonas quae circuerunt caelos".*

27 The Evernew Tongue replied: "The seven heavens around the world about which you enquire are these: In the first place, the bright radiant heaven with clouds which is nearest to you, from which shines the moon and the scattering of stars. There are two gleaming sparkling heavens above this, containing an abundance of angels, and the spreading winds. Above these is a cold icy heaven, bluer than every bright colour, seven times colder than snow. From this the sun shines. Above that are two further beautiful bright heavens from which shine the fiery constellations which bring fruitfulness to the sea. There is a fiery great heaven over these, the highest of them all, on which the heavenly orbit is set. It is a sunny blazing heaven, in which work consists of musical harmony and choral singing of angels".

28 "In the zones of the seven heavens are hidden the twelve quivering animals, in their heavenly bodies, topped with fiery heads, which blow twelve winds around the world. In the same zones sleep the dragons with fiery breath, towering-headed dragons with diseased sides, which set in motion the rumbling of thunder, and emit flashes

of lightning from the pupils of their eyes. Zones circle around heaven",
he told them," and heaven has seven orbits around the earth".

29 "In the first place, there is a cold icy zone where seas are assumed
under the surface of the northerly part of heaven. There is another cold
icy zone which links together the beasts under the sea and those under
the southern side of the world, in the place where were set the nine
fiery pillars to the south of heaven. There is a splendid noble zone of
the world which nourishes the many fruits of the earth until they rise
up around the world from its depths in the west. There are two other
beautiful mild zones in which is the foment which produces heat and
cold, and causes many afflictions on the surface of the earth on all
sides".

30 *"Aibne fisen asbae fribae flanis lia sieth*: On the third day God created
lakes and many seas, various kinds of waters, and many forms of salt
sea, as well as the circumference of the earth, with its level lands and
mountains, its woodlands, its precious stones, and its varied trees".

31 *Interrogauerunt sapientes Ebriorum: "Indica nobis multa genera et misteria
maris".* The Evernew Tongue replied: "There are three oceans of sea
around the world. In the first place is a sea with seven forms under the
sides of the earth, against which hell rumbles, and raises a noise
around the valley. A limpid blue salt sea surrounds the world on all
sides, which sets flood and ebb in motion, and casts up many fruit. The
third ocean is a flaming sea. From the heavens are sent forth nine
winds which arouse it from its slumber. Its waves sing four hundred
and seventy melodies after it has been awakened. In its wave-call it
resounds like thunder. From the beginning of the world it does not
cease from flooding, yet it is never at full tide except on Sunday. On
Sunday it falls asleep, until the sound of the winds awake with the
coming on Sunday of God from heaven, and with the harmony of the
angels above it. ..".

32 The Evernew Tongue was heard to say: *"Alea fas uide nistien alme ama
faus elobi reba*: On the fourth day God created the seventy-two kinds
of stars which traverse heaven, along with the fiery orbit of the sun,
which heats the world with the swiftness of the wind, and with the
skill and splendour of angels. It illuminates twelve plains along the

earth's sides. Its light every night makes a circuit by which the fiery sea is warmed, and at which hosts of angels rejoice...".

33   *Interrogauerunt sapientes Ebreorum:* "Tell us about the twelve plains beneath the earth's sides, for which the sun shines to give light every night, for we are ignorant of this knowledge".

34   The Evernew Tongue replied: "This is where the sun goes at sun-set every night: In the first place it illuminates the transmarine river and the eastern part of the oceans. Then it lights up the great fiery sea at night, and the sulphurous seas around the red lands. Then it shines on the hosts of youths in the playing fields, who cry out to heaven in fear of the beast which kills many thousands of people under the waves to the south. Thereafter it illuminates the mountain with streams of fire which traverse the earthen plains with their accompanying hosts. Then it shines on the lair of the whale whom the twenty-four champions oppose, responding [from] the valley of pain.

35   After that it shines in front of the fearsome fence enclosing the host of hell in the north. It shines in the dark valleys with the plaintive streams on their surfaces. Then it illuminates the lair of the beast which conveys the many seas around the sides of the earth in every direction, and which sucks in the seas again, leaving dry shores on every side. It shines, moreover, on the fiery mountain formed from the fire of doom for the destruction of every created thing. It shines on the many thousands who, from the beginning of the world, sleep the sad sleep in the valley of the flowers. It illuminates the sorrowful tearful plain with the dragons placed in its gloom. Then it lights up the flocks of birds which sing together the many melodies in the valleys of the flowers. It shines on the radiant plains with the bright flowers which illuminate the valley. Finally it shines in the direction of Adam's Paradise until it rises again from the east in the morning...".

36   *"Alimbea fones arife aste.boia fiten salmibia libe lib ebile nab lea fabe:* On the fifth day God created the seventy-two kinds of bird-flocks, and the seventy-two kinds of beasts of the sea. Each species had its own particular form, habits, and nature.

37   Firstly, there are the birds of the island of Naboth. There has not shone

on earth a colour or radiance which does not shine from their wings. They shed tears in cold and snow. They rejoice in the heat and brightness of summer. They awaken always at midnight, and sing melodies sweet as harpstrings.

38 As for the birds of Sabes, their wings shine at night-time like lighted candles. Any affliction which is touched by their wings or by their shadow when in flight is cured. They assume a torpid inertia in the season of winter and cold, and they awaken at May-day. In their slumbers they sing gentle music like the sound of wind.

39 There are the birds of Abuad, in the islands between the east of Africa and the heavens. There has not appeared on earth a beautiful colour which has not radiated from their wings, and no feather or plumage has fallen from them since the beginning of the world, yet the amount of their plumage has not increased. The fragrance and scent of flowers, and the taste of the seven rivers of wine which traverse the bright plains is what suffices them for food since the creation. They do not cease from singing in harmony, and they are not wearied until midnight brings the chant of the angels from a cloud.

40 The three bird-flocks are distributed thus, seventy thousand and seventy-two birds in each flock. At midnight the first flock raises its cry. It praises God by means of its song, and tells of the wonderful innumerable mysteries created by the Lord from the beginning of the world to Doomsday.

41 At the end of the night comes the final bird-flock. With sevenfold melody it tells of the din to descend on the world with the fear of Doomsday. Then it will relate the seventy-fold division of punishment to those who merit it, and will describe the seventy-two seats in the heavenly mansions for all who deserve them.

42 *Et diresir alba sibe alea me lis:* If the race of Adam should hear the music of those birds, they would not be parted from the sound gladly or with pleasure, but rather with grief, longing, and sadness, until they die from weeping.

43 *Efi lia lasien ferosa filera leus dissia nimbile nue bua faune intoria tebnae, id*

est: Faciamus hominem ad imaginem et ad similitudinem nostram, et praesit piscibus mariss et uolatilibus celi et bestis uniuersae terrae.

44   Such is the bountiful power of the Lord that, after the trespass, there were twenty-four types among Adam's descendants".

24. *TRANSITUS MARIAE*

1   On a certain occasion, Mary, mother of the Lord, was chanting her psalms, and praying, having completed forty-seven years since the Saviour had ascended to heaven. It was then that Christ, son of the living God, came from the angels of heaven to seek out Mary, his mother, and he said: "O Mary, take this palm in your hand, since the end of your life is drawing near, and I think it time to bring you to everlasting rest. I will, indeed, send all the apostles to meet your body, and they will not part from you until you are borne into the heavenly kingdom of repose and eternal joy".

2   Then Mary took the palm from her son, and said: "This palm which you gave me, beloved son, once people see that I have it, their anger and envy will rise against me". Jesus then said to Mary: "Do not be afraid or fearful of taking the palm from me, since great wonders and miracles will be performed through it in Jerusalem".

3   When Mary heard those words she took the palm in her hand, and the Saviour went towards the beautiful Mount Olivet, and as he drew near the mountain she saw a shining image like a fire upon the Mount. And then, as Christ and his holy mother traversed the mountain, all of its trees bowed down on every side about the paths and ways which they were traversing, lowering their topmost branches and adoring the resplendent palm held by the Virgin Mary. Thereupon Mary rejoiced greatly, and she said to Jesus: "It is evident that all the trees are adoring you and honouring the palm which is in my hand. And now it is clearly manifest to me that you are Christ, son of the living God, come from heaven to find me, since nobody else has power to do these things, but you yourself, Jesus ". Christ said to Mary: "Did you not, on a former occasion, see my miracle at the time when you and Joseph went into Egypt in flight from Herod ? You came to the desert in which this palm was, along with the other trees. You said to Joseph: 'We are hungry and we now have nothing to eat in this desert to which we have come'. I was then an innocent child in your arms. Joseph told you then that he

had nothing to relieve your hunger except the fruit on the palm which he saw standing alone in the desert. Joseph said: 'None of these trees has any fruit save the palm-tree alone, and I cannot climb that on account of its height. I advise you to breast-feed your son lest he be hungry along with us. As we are convinced that the child was conceived through the power of the Holy Spirit, may the Holy Spirit save him from hunger, and may he show mercy to us who will rear him'. Then, O mother, Joseph said to you in the desert where the three of us were on Mount Olivet: 'Great is my hunger'. I, a child in your arms, said to Joseph: 'What, dear father, prevents you from climbing the tree to get the fruit for my mother to eat? Believe this, and all that I tell you, since it is I who will nourish you, and everyone in the world. Indeed, none of all those who will believe in me will go hungry'. And then, dear mother, the infant in your arms turned to face the palm-tree and said to it: 'Bend down your upper branches'. It bowed down immediately. I said to it: 'O greatest of the trees of Egypt, arise and raise your noble and honourable branches before me, by virtue of the generous obedience which you showed me in the desert. With that, the palm rose up before you and ascended into the air and into the firmament, and was deposited in Paradise'. Who else, O Virgin Mary, would have moved the palm but I alone?" asked he. "I bless those who do homage to God, and I will place them in the abode of the just when their souls leave their bodies. I have reminded you just now of these things, O mother Mary, lest you disbelieve the arrangements I make through my miraculous power. When your soul leaves your body I will come again to seek you, with a legion of angels and all the apostles in my company, as I have promised you already, and they will be praying over your body, and I will assuredly hear that prayer". When Christ had said these words to Mary and departed, Mary then sat down, and Jesus understood that she was filled with sadness and dejection. He came again to bring her solace, and her heart was filled with the joy of the Holy Spirit when the Saviour came into her presence. And Mary said to Jesus: "Extend your goodness to the apostles also, for at the end of time there will be false apostles and false teaching, and you will hear them."

4   Then Christ went to heaven, and Mary proceeded to her own house. As she drew near, a thunderous shaking seized the whole house in acknowledgement of the glory and honour of the palm which had

formerly been in the hand of Jesus. She went into the innermost recess of the house and bathed and dressed in honour of the creator who had been speaking to her. And she sat down and began to bless her son, saying to him: "I bless you for having come on earth to me from heaven. I bless all who are in heaven praising you constantly. I bless you for having chosen me in heaven, and for having accepted my body on earth. I bless you for bringing me into the heavenly kingdom. My soul and light will be in the midst of the angels of heaven because you have come to me. [And I bless] all the deeds which you have done, since they will endure forever, and the devil will have no power over me".

5   After Mary had said these words, the heavenly father sent tidings and messengers to her pious and trustworthy neighbours. When they came to her, she said to them: "Let you all listen to me, for the reason you have been gathered to me is that tomorrow my spirit will leave me, and will go to the eternal kingdom. Until then, let you look after me, for it is not gold or silver which I seek from you but fervent prayers. Attend well at my death, and prepare me for burial, and let each of you carry a shining lamp, since that is better than lamenting and bewailing the transience of the world. I, for my part, will be as a star contending with the devil who is engaged in the destruction of the human race. I assure you that the devil has no power over the just, for two angels come to meet the soul of every person at the hour of death, the angel of righteousness, and the angel of unrighteousness. If a person performs good deeds while alive, the angel of righteousness will come for his soul, and will take it to the abode of the just. However, if a person does evil, the inhabitants of hell along with the devil will come for him. Dear brothers and sisters", said Mary, "let us ensure that that the devil has no dwelling amongst us, and that he has no power over us".

6   Great trembling and fear seized the virgins when they heard those words of Mary, and they said: "O pre-eminent among the human race, and mother of the saviour, if you who are our protector are in fear of the devil, how shall we face him? For if the shepherd flees before the wolf, where shall the sheep go?" When they had said this, they began to weep and grieve in the presence of Mary and all who were in the house. Then Mary said to them: "Be silent and do not disobey the Lord". They all rose immediately and prayed to the Lord, and related

Christ's wonder-working and miracles in the presence of Mary.

7	As they were speaking thus, John the Evangelist entered the place where Mary was, and when Mary saw John she sighed aloud deeply and could not restrain her grieving and sorrow. She said: "Beloved father, John, do you remember how the holy Saviour entrusted me to you on the day he was crucified for the sake of the human race ? On that day you were before him, and I said to him: ' It is evident where you are going. To whom do you commend me, and in whose company are you leaving me?' 'I leave you in John's company, and I entrust you to his care'. "And do you remember, O John, the charge which Christ gave to me of you? For you were trustworthy among the apostles, and it was you who slept alongside him on the final night." Then John replied to Mary and said: "What do you wish your disciple to do?" Mary answered John, and said to him: "I ask only that you be at my death-bed, and that you watch over my body, and do not allow me to go to heaven unattended. I myself heard some of the Jews proclaim that they would burn my body when my soul should depart from me, saying that they would [thus] be doing the will of the Jewish people".

8	Now when John heard that it was on the following day that Mary was to go to heaven, he prostrated himself on the ground and wept bitterly, moistening the earth in front of him. "O Lord of mercy", said he," why do you permit us to suffer the tribulations and distresses of this world, since we are not able to endure them?". Mary said to John: "Arise and cease your weeping and sorrowing". And she ordered those who were in the house to rise and chant their psalms, while she conversed and spoke with John before her death.

9	Then Mary took John with her to the back of the house to an unfre-quented place, and she told him of the clothes which she had prepared for her burial, and she said to him: "You know that I own none of the garments in my house except my burial-garments and these two tunics which are for the two virgins who are here with me. I leave these as a bequest to them ". Then Mary showed John the palm which the Saviour gave to her, and she said to him: "I ask you, dear John, that you take this palm from me and that you place it over my burial-site when my soul leaves me".

10 John then answered Mary and said to her: "I cannot take this palm until there has been a council of all the other apostles about it, lest there should be envy or jealousy among the others on account of its being given to me in preference to all of them, for among the apostles there is one who is closer to God than me by virtue of order [of instution]. Let all the apostles come in his company to this place, so that they may pay you the honour to which you are entitled, as your son commanded them".

11 After John had said these words, at that hour and time all the apostles came from the various districts and cities where they had been preaching the gospel. And they came out of the clouds of heaven to the door of the house where the Virgin Mary was. Then there was a tumult in the elements because of the assembling of all the apostles to come to Mary's house. The first to enter was the apostle Peter, the head of the Church, and after him was Paul, the vessel of election, he who, most of all, had led contemporaries to the faith. And when each of them saw the other he was amazed to see his companion. Each in turn greeted the other, and they said:"We give thanks to our heavenly Lord that he has such love for us that he has brought us together to the same place, since it is thus that the prophecy of the chief prophet, the son of Joseph , is fulfilled, when he said these words: '*Ecce quam bonum et quam iocundum habitare fratres in unum*'. 'What is more delightful than a gathering of the holy brothers' ". And all the apostles said: "Let us pray to our Lord that he may reveal to us why were brought here".

12 Then the apostle Peter answered them, and said to Paul: "Let you pray first to the powerful Lord". Paul replied to Peter: "How could I pray to the Lord in your presence, for I am the apostle who was latest to be chosen among you all ? It is not fitting for me to pray the Lord before you. However, O Peter, you are the greatest and most senior of all the apostles", said Paul. "Let you pray to the Lord on our behalf and on your own. Which of us would venture to make intercession to the Lord when you are present?" Thereupon all the apostles were filled with great joy because of Paul's plea.

13 Then Peter said: "Let us all in unison beseech Jesus, the son of the living God [to reveal] why it was granted to us [to be in] this place". Thus he prayed, lowering his face to the ground, and bending his knees, and

he began and said: "O God almighty", he said, "we are in your orders on heaven and on earth, you who defeated the devil and brought his power to nought, and performed [this] wonder. For you are our everlasting strength and our firm expectation, Father, Son, and Holy Spirit, who existed, and exists , through the ages forever". Then all the apostles responded to Peter and echoed his words.

14   Then John came toward them and said: "Bless me, dear brothers", said he. Peter and Andrew came and replied to John, saying: "Dear John, our best-loved among the human race, tell us how you arrived here". John replied, saying "When I was in the city called Ephesus in the south-east of the world in the territories of Asia Minor, preaching with a company of twenty-nine, a great cloud in the air came towards us, and I heard the voice of the Saviour in the cloud above. And we were raised up and brought here, to the house of the Virgin Mary and to all the holy people ". Thus he conversed with the apostles, and said: "Dear brothers, Mary's death is close at hand. Let there be no weeping or sorrow among us, so that there may be no murmuring or perturbation among the people, but let each of you unite together praising the Lord. For Jesus Christ enjoined on me on his final night that there should be no sadness or grief when one of us should go to heaven".

15-17 Then John and the apostles entered the house where Mary was, and said to her: *Aue Maria gracia* ..."Hail to thee, Virgin Mary, filled with the grace of the Holy Spirit. Blessed is the fruit of thy womb". Mary answered, saying: "May God be with you. Pray tell me, O apostles of the Lord, how you have come here, or who has told you that I am near death?" The apostles then told her: "The power of the Lord transported each of us in the clouds of heaven from the places where we were spreading the word of God". Thereupon Mary rejoiced greatly at the words of the apostles, and began to bless her son, saying: " My blessing on you, O son, lord of all creation. Now is the fulfillment of all your recent promise to me, that you would send the apostles to my obsequies".

18   Then Mary took them to the inner part of the house and showed them her burial-garments and her shroud. On the beginning of the third day, the final end of death drew near to Mary.

19-21 And Peter said to all the apostles: "Let each man of you hold a lighted lamp in his hand, so that we may be worthy before the Saviour, and let none of you say that this is Mary's death, but rather [her] everlasting life and eternal glory". Then Paul said to Peter: " Dear father, do you know that I have never seen the Saviour in the flesh since I became a believer, and I would like Christ to reveal to me some of the teachings and the miracles which he revealed to you on Mount Olivet". "Dear father Paul," said Peter, "wait yet, for Christ will come to us for Mary's body. For everything he ever promised us has been well fulfilled". Paul then said to Peter: "If you wish to make known the teaching of God to me, tell me some of your own teachings, so that I may follow them for as long as I live". Peter said to Paul: "O Paul", said he, " what you seek is good. This is the teaching: ' He who does not fast every day will not attain the kingdom of God' ". Paul said: "Dear father Peter", said he, " do not say that, for the people will not accept such teaching because of its severity. They will rise up against you, and will kill you, and will do the devil's service". Then Paul turned to John and asked him how he would present the teaching so that the people would accept it. John replied, saying: "He who does not avoid all evil will not attain the kingdom of heaven". Paul said to John: "The people will give a bad reception to that teaching, and will threaten to stone you on account of the difficulty of the admonition". Then Paul said to Andrew: "How shall the teaching be expounded?" Andrew replied, saying: "He who does not leave father and mother and sister and all his friends for love of the Saviour will not see the kingdom of heaven". Paul then said: "The teaching of John and of Peter is easier than that, Andrew. The people of the present time will not accept that difficult counsel, for just as too great a burden is not be placed on an unbroken horse, so also one should not make excessive demands on the people until they acquire judgement". Peter then said: "Dear brother Paul, how do you wish the teaching to be set forth?" Paul replied, saying: "I seek from the mighty Lord [the revelation] of how to teach in a manner that the people will be receptive to me, that is, by setting forth tolerable admonitions, such as that everyone should fast once a week. In this way, they will not be overcome by fatigue or weariness". Then a great rumbling came towards the apostles from the clouds of heaven. It was Christ, the son of the living God, the saviour of the race of Adam, who was coming from the sun-filled mansions of heaven, accompanied by Michael the Archangel and his [angelic] orders. They descended silently and noiselessly in the midst of the apostles, whom Christ greeted, saying: "Hail, dear apostles. I tell you that your teaching, as you have propounded it, will not be accepted, but the teaching of Paul will". And Christ asked the apostles: "Why not free the whole world from the snares and traps of the devil? You should present lenient teaching to the people so that it will be accepted from you, for it is at the end of time that such teaching will have its fulfillment". Then Christ said to Paul: "Do not be saddened or grieved that the apostles do not reveal the divine mysteries to you, for I will reveal them to you and to Mary". Then Christ departed in a shining flame, and called Paul to him. When Judas saw Christ taking Paul with him to heaven he said: "O Jesus, son of the living God, you came in human form into this world, and for that reason people are not free to move (from it) except according to the merits of each. Why, then, are you taking with you to heaven this man, Paul, without his fighting against me to attain heaven as did the other apostles?" "Let him come here", said the devil, "so that we may fight, and find out which of us is the stronger. And if strength is on his side, take him with you to heaven, and show him all the pains in hell and the glory of heaven". Jesus said to Paul: "Arise and do battle, for I have promised to bring to heaven only those who overcome the devil". Christ said to Peter: "Rise up with Paul, and let you both join combat with the devil". The two then went and fought the devil, who fell at their hands.

22-23 Paul and Peter then came along with the other apostles to the house in which the Virgin Mary was, and no man in the world could look on Mary because of the radiance which surrounded her. Then a great voice came from heaven and said to them: "My strength and my power and I myself will be with you until the end and consummation of the world". Mary and the apostles, on hearing the voice of the Saviour, replied aloud : "We bless you , O Lord, who guides and governs every soul". Then Mary went to make intercession to the Lord, and when she had completed her prayers she entered the house, and lay on her bed. All the apostles were around her. It was the hour after mid-day. Then the house was filled with a great sound and with the fragrance of angels, so that everyone who was inside fell asleep to the strains of angelic music, except the apostles and the virgins. Mary ordered these to say their prayers.

24   Thereupon Christ, son of the living God, came with the angels of heaven, who were singing heavenly harmonies for the Saviour, and in honour of Mary. Christ greeted the apostles, and Mary saluted him, saying: "I bless you, son of the heavenly father. You have fulfilled all your promises, and have come yourself [for me]".

25-27   When Mary had finished saying these words, the spirit of life departed from her, and the Saviour took it in his hands with reverence and honour. The archangels of heaven rose up around her, and the apostles saw her being raised up by the angels, in human form, and seven times brighter than the sun. Then the apostles enquired whether there was any other soul as bright as the soul of Mary. Jesus answered, and said to Peter: "All souls are like that after baptism. When in the world, the darkness of bodily sin adheres to them. No one else in the world is able to avoid sin as Mary could, therefore Mary's soul is brighter than the soul of every other person in the world".

28   Then Jesus said to Peter: "Put her shroud around the body of Mary, and take it to the left side of the city, for there is the burial-place of Anna, her own mother. Place her in that grave and watch over it, as I have ordered you". As Jesus had said these words, the body of Mary spoke and said: "Are you mindful, O Lord, of the full preservation of my remains, according to prophecy?" Jesus replied to Mary's body and said to her: "I will not leave you", said he, "since you were my temple of safe-keeping, O eternal mother, the pure treasury in which the body of the Lord was conceived". When Christ had completed this eulogy of his mother, Mary ascended to heaven.

29-31   Then Peter and the other apostles, and the three virgins who were looking after the body of Mary, took away the remains of the holy mother of the Lord with the dignity which she deserved.

32-35   Peter took the palm and said to John: "Dear father," said he, " since you are the youngest among us, bear the palm before us, and commence the praise of the Lord". John replied to Peter: "You are our father, our chief apostle, our teacher, and the head of the holy Church. Let you precede us". Then Peter rose and began the psalm. Thus was the soul of Mary borne in the midst of angels into the clouds of heaven, and her body on earth borne by the apostles to its burial-place.

36-37 When the Jewish people and an impious leader of the priests heard the apostles chanting their psalms over the body of Mary, and the weeping of her friends lamenting her, then the leader of the Jewish priests rose up, [incited by] the attacker of the human race, the upholder of every evil and obstructor of every good. He said to his people: "Let the apostles be slain, and the body of Mary burnt, since it was she who bore the deceiver who came amongst you". The Jewish people came then with venomous swords and broad harshly-pointed spears to kill the apostles.

38 Thereupon their sight was banished from their eyes, and strength from their hands, and movement from their feet, so that the Jews had no means of guidance as to where whey should go.

39 Yet the power of the devil was [still] among them, so that one of them sprang violently forward to break the palm which was in the hand of John, the beloved disciple, and to knock down the body of Mary from the bier on which it lay. He stretched his hands towards the bier. Indeed he did not fail to grasp it, for his hands separated from his body and adhered to the bier.

40-44 Then the Jew shrieked and cried most piteously, and began to beseech the Lord and the apostles to help him. Peter answered him and said: "If you believe that it is Jesus who can save you, you will be healed in body and in mind by him". "I believe", said he, "that it was Jesus whom our faith rejected when we crucified him out of jealousy and envy". Peter said: "If you believe wholeheartedly, go and greet Mary, and kiss the bier on which her body lies. Then you will be made whole". The Jew did as Peter told him, and he was healed through the miracles of Mary and the apostles because he made fervent repentance.

45-46 Then Peter said to the Jew: "Take this palm in your hand and go into the city. Let everyone who has lost the use of eyes, hands or feet affirm belief in Jesus Christ, son of the living God. Then touch them with the palm, and they will be made whole through the miracles of God". Following Peter's instruction, he went to the Jewish people, and told them how he had been healed, and said to them: "Everyone who believes as I believed will be made well". The people of the city did as they were advised, and they recovered, and believed in God and in the apostles.

47 Then the apostles took the body of Mary to be buried, and placed themselves around the grave as Christ had commanded them. Thereafter Jesus came with the angels of heaven along with him, and said to them: "My peace and strength and power be with you", he said.

48 Michael then told his company to raise up the body of Mary into the clouds. As the angels lifted up the body, Christ said to the apostles : "Come up close to me".

49 And thus they went to heaven along with the Saviour, who said to them: "Go to Adam's paradise". When the apostles reached Paradise they found the body of Mary before them, under the tree of life. Her soul was restored again to her body .

50 Then the apostles said to Jesus:"Once upon a time when we were with you we asked to have hell shown to us". And Jesus said to them: "You will be the worse for seeing it"."We will not leave you without a sight of it", they said. "You promised to reveal it to us on the day when Mary's body came to its resting-place.Then Jesus said to them: "I will show hell to you if that is your wish". " It is, indeed", they said. When they had ceased speaking a great cloud came to them, which bore the apostles and Michael and the Virgin Mary along with the Saviour to the entrance of hell.They were lowered to the ground there, and Jesus said: "Let hell be opened for us". And it was opened immediately.

51 When the inhabitants of hell saw Jesus before them, with the apostles, Mary and Michael, they began to weep, and said: "O Michael, you are our ruler, and we look to you to act on our behalf".When the apostles saw the pains of hell , they could not bear to look further at them.Then Michael turned his face to the ground, and wept bitterly. And he said: "I feel as if I myself am suffering those pains". Jesus said to Michael: "Rise up and stop your weeping, for those people are not dearer to you than to their maker, nor is your mercy more far-reaching than is his". "O Michael", said Jesus," you are not justified in what you say, for I offered my body and blood for their sakes.You, however, O Michael, are praying for them only for the space of a single hour", said Jesus.

52   Then Jesus said: "Go, Michael, and show the apostles some of the pains
     of hell". Michael pointed out to them people with fiery lumps in their
     mouths, who could not speak except to groan as they suffered their
     pain. Peter asked Michael: "What evil was performed by those who are
     in this state?" Michael answered and said: "They are learned men who
     did not themselves fulfill the teaching which they enjoined on all
     others". They saw other people in great pain, with their hands per-
     petually ablaze , unable to look up to seek help, with little burning
     leeches sucking at their thighs. " What evil did that group do?", asked
     Peter. Michael answered and said:"They are the priests who under-
     stand neither the words of God nor the canons of the Lord , though
     they receive the Lord's body, and who lack understanding of the
     words of penance to be said over those who confess to them".

53   The apostles saw other people with burning fetters on their hands and
     legs, being scourged by demons. [They asked] what evil these had
     done. [They were told]: "These were impious elders who had much
     worldly wealth, yet never gave any in alms to the poor, but let it go
     from them in unprofitable ventures.For that reason they suffer such
     pains". Then the apostles saw others with red-hot flaming swords
     through their tongues. "What wrong-doing have these committed?",
     asked Peter."They are unjust judges who falsify decisions in order to
     receive rewards or preferment", said Michael.

54   Jesus and Mary came to them then and asked Michael to cease to point
     out the pains of hell. When the inhabitants of hell saw Mary and Christ
     they lamented, saying: "O Mary, mother of the illustrious one, implore
     your son to grant us relief from our pains". Christ answered them and
     said: "I was crucified for your sakes, my side was pierced, and a crown
     [of thorns] placed on my head. You, however, rejected the ten com-
     mandments of the law of God , in defiance of my teaching. Why,
     therefore, should I grant you a respite?" Then Mary knelt on the
     ground, bared her right breast, and shed copious tears on the earth ,
     beseeching her son to come to the aid of those in hell. Then Christ said:
     "In honour of Mary, of the apostles, and of Michael, I will grant them
     a respite from their pains for three hours every Sunday". Then Jesus
     said: "Let you close hell". They closed hell at his command.

55   The body of Mary was placed under the tree of life in Paradise, with
      a heavenly host alongside, praising the Lord eternally.The apostles,
      having left Mary with Jesus, went to their own lands to spread the
      word of God.

25. IRISH TEXT OF *Visio Sancti Pauli*

1 "This concerns Sunday, the day chosen by God, when angels and archangels are most joyous. The matter in question here is, who is the person who asked God that the souls of sinners receive on Sunday a greater respite than on any other day of the week? It is said that it was the apostle Paul, and Michael the archangel, when they went to see hell. For God had wished Paul to see the punishments of hell, and he sent Michael the archangel along with him, and the tortures of hell were revealed to him".

2 "In front of the entrance to hell Paul saw a fiery tree, on the branches of which many sinners' souls were being tortured and crucified. Some of them were were hanging by their hair, some by the neck, others by the hands and feet, others still by their tongues. Then he saw a pit of fire, ablaze with seven flames, with extraordinary heat in every one of them. There were many souls being punished in this. He saw seven tortures, moreover, round about the pit. The first of these was snow, the second, ice, the third, fire, the fourth, blood, the fifth, serpents, the sixth, thunder, the seventh, stench. In that pit were the souls of sinners who did not do penance in this life. Some of them were crying, wailing, and groaning, others sought death, without getting it, for the soul never dies".

3 "In that case, dear brethren", said the sage, "there is reason to fear the place where there is perpetual disease, grief without joy, heartfelt sighs, and abundance of tears. There is a wheel with a thousand spokes, and every day it is struck a thousand times by the devil, and a thousand souls are tortured on each one of these occasions. There is an odious brown river, in which there are a thousand demonic beasts, like fish from the depths of the sea, which mercilessly swallow the souls of sinners like a wolf devours sheep. There is a bridge over that river, over which the righteous souls pass without stumbling. And all [other] souls which traverse it attain an end in accordance with their own deeds. There are many other terrible dwellings prepared for

132

burning the sinners. And like is along with like there, adulterers with other adulterers, thieves with other thieves, the unrighteous with other unrighteous people. The manner in which each one gets across the bridge over the river is relative to his own actions".

4 Thereafter Paul saw many other dwellings in which innumerable souls were being punished, some up to their knees, some up to their navels, others to their necks, others still, up to their eyebrows, being done to death in that torture. Paul wept and sighed greatly at the sight, and he asked Michael: "Who are those suffering that pain up to their knees and up to their navels?" The angel replied that those in pain to their knees were those who indulge in idle gossip and backbiting about their neighbours. Those in pain to their navels were adulterers who did not repent until the time of death. Those in pain up to their mouths were those church-goers who do not listen attentively to the words of God. Those in pain up to the eyebrows were those who rejoice and delight in their neighbours' ruin.

5 Then Paul saw another place, full of men and women who were consuming their own tongues, and he asked Michael: "Who are these?" Michael said: "They are usurers who exacted interest mercilessly".

6. Paul saw yet another place then, in which were maidens in black, clad in garments of pitch and fiery sulphor, with serpents, toads, and other horrible creatures around their necks, and four demons with fiery horns surrounding them, and torturing them. They were saying: "We acknowledge you, O Son of the Heavenly Father, who redeemed the descendants of Adam with your own blood". Paul asked Michael: "Who are the people in this state?" Michael replied that they were young girls who were not chaste at the time of marriage, who had committed fornication with their own fathers and brothers, who avoided having infants, or who killed the infants, leaving them to be consumed by animals, or throwing them into water to be drowned".

7 Thereafter he saw men and women in a cold icy place, with fire burning them from behind, and cold in their faces perishing them. Paul asked Michael: "Who are these?" He replied: "They are those who revile and put to shame widows and poor people".

8   He then saw men and women at the water's edge, suffering from thirst
      and hunger, with much ripe fruit in front of them, but they could not
      taste it. Paul asked Michael who was in this condition. Michael said:
      "Those are people who did not fast or abstain at the proper time".

9   They also saw elderly men weeping and lamenting in the midst of four
      demons who were torturing them. Paul asked Michael: "Who are
      these?" He replied: "They are impious bishops who did not fulfil the
      law of God, who were not chaste in their bodies, and who were
      covetous, haughty, and envious in word and thought. For these
      reasons they suffer these immeasurable torments until the Day of
      Judgement". Paul wept then, and said: "Woe to the sinners that they
      were ever born". And Michael said to him: "Why do you weep? For
      you have not yet seen the greatest punishments in hell".

10   Then Michael showed Paul a fearful pit, and said to him: "Remain
      standing here, and endure what you hear as best you can". Paul did
      this. The pit was wide open, and a horrible fetid stench rose from it,
      which exceeded all the pains of hell in its awfulness. Michael said to
      Paul: "Whoever is put in that pit will never be in the presence of God
      either before or after the Judgement". Paul asked Michael: "Who is
      consigned there?" Michael said that they were those who did not
      believe that Christ was crucified to save the race of Adam, those who
      did not receive the body of Christ, those who did not believe that the
      Son of God was born of the Virgin, those who did not accept baptism
      or blessing, and those who did not commemorate in communion the
      body and blood of Jesus Christ.

11   Thereafter Paul saw another place in which naked men and women
      were being consumed by horrible serpents. They were piled closely on
      top of each other like sheep in a pen. The place seemed to him to be as
      deep as the space from heaven to earth. He heard them crying and
      groaning, and later he saw them, away in the distance from him. He
      saw the soul of a sinner in the grasp of seven devils on the day that it
      was taken from the body. Then angels rose up and said to it: "Alas, for
      you, O soul, that you acted evilly in the world, for you insulted God
      on earth". The soul itself held and read the scroll on which were its
      sins. Then the devils seized it, and consigned it to the dreadful
      dwellings of furthest hell. Afterwards the angel said to Paul: "Believe

and understand, O Paul, that everyone is assigned a place here according to his deserts".

12   In a single short instant Paul saw a righteous soul, after its departure from the body, being brought to heaven. And he heard the sound of a thousand angels saying: "O fortunate chosen soul who has upheld the law of God, you are entitled to rejoice, for you did the will of God on earth". The angels that were conveying the soul said that it should be raised up before the devil to read out its own good deeds. The souls of sinners inside in hell cried out, saying: "Have mercy on us, Michael and Paul. Implore the King of heaven and earth to have pity on us, for we understand that it was he who redeemed us". Michael said: "Let you weep, and, along with you, Paul and I will ask with tears that you be granted mercy". When the devils in hell heard this, they cried out loudly, saying: "Have mercy on us, O Son of the living God".

13   The laments were heard in heaven, and God said: "Why did you not do good when alive, since you are now asking for my mercy? I was crucified for your sakes, my blood was spilt, nails were driven through me, and I was given gall and vinegar to drink. Thus I was made to suffer the Passion on your account, yet you were evil, deceitful, proud, and envious. You did not give alms or fast or do penance in return for this".

14   Then Michael and Paul knelt down before the King of heaven and earth, asking that everyone who was in hell should receive mercy from God every Sunday. When Christ heard this he said: "On account of the appeal of Mary, Michael and Paul, and the other saints besides, and out of my own goodness, I grant them a respite from vespers on Saturday to the third hour of prime on Monday".

15   When the souls in hell heard that, they rejoiced and called out aloud, saying: "We acknowledge that you are the Son of the living God, you who have granted this succour to us on a Sunday, for this is greater help to us than our being alive. Those who do not observe Sunday will not receive a place in the company of the angels of God".

16   Paul asked Michael how many punishments were in hell. Michael said: "Even if the men of the world from the beginning of time to the

Day of Judgement were to enumerate them, and if every one of them had a hundred tongues, even so, they could not reckon the extent of the punishments of hell".

17   "Therefore, beloved brothers and sisters, be instructed to do good deeds, to protect yourselves from the pain of hell, so you may be brought to your own Lord, the King of heaven and earth. For those who do not believe in him, and do not do penance for their sins, will be consigned to the punishments which we have related".

26. THE VISION OF ADOMNÁN

1   Noble and wonderful is the Lord of the elements, and great and
marvellous his strength and power. He is kind, gentle, merciful, and
benevolent. For he invites to heaven those who are charitable, compas-
sionate, humane, and clement. However, he lays low and casts down
to hell the impious, worthless company of the damned. He provides
the mysteries and varied rewards of heaven for the blessed, and the
manifold diversity of pain for the sons of death.

2   There are very many saints and righteous followers of the Lord of the
elements, as well as apostles and disciples of Jesus Christ, to whom the
mysteries and secrets of the kingdom of heaven, and the glorious
rewards of the just, have thereby been revealed, and to whom have
been revealed also the various tortures of hell, and those who suffer
them. The four-cornered ship let down from heaven with four ropes
was manifested to the apostle Peter. Its sound was as sweet as any
music. The apostle Paul was raised up to the third heaven, where he
heard the unutterable words of the angels, and the wonderful conversation of the people of heaven. Moreover, on the day of the death of
Mary, all the apostles were brought to see the pains and pitiable
tortures of the wretched, when the Lord ordered the angels of sunset
to open the earth before the apostles, so that they might see and
contemplate hell with its many torments, as he himself had promised
them long before his crucifixion.

3   Finally, the revelation was made to the present subject of discussion,
Adomnán, grandson of Tinne, the great scholar of the western world.
When his soul departed from his body on the feast of John the Baptist,
he was taken to the heavenly kingdom with its angels, and to hell with
its rabble. When his soul left the body, the angel who accompanied
him when he was alive immediately appeared, and took him first to
see the kingdom of heaven.

4   The first land they reached was the Land of the Saints. That is a fertile

lustrous land. There are various splendid companies there, wearing cloaks of bright linen with resplendent hoods over their heads. The saints of the eastern world are in their own particular assembly in the east of the Land of the Saints. The saints of the western world are in the west of the same land. Moreover, the saints of the northerly and southerly parts of the world are in two great assemblies to the south and to the north. Yet, everyone in the Land of the Saints is equally near, so as to hear the music, and contemplate the place in which are the nine heavenly orders, ranged according to their dignity and rank.

5   Sometimes the saints sing wonderful music in praise of God, At other times, they listen to the music of the host of heaven. For the saints have no need of anything other than to be listening to the music which they hear, contemplating the radiance which they see, and being pleased by the fragrance of the land.

6   There is a splendid kingdom facing them to the south-east, with a golden porch to the south of it, separated from them by a crystal screen. It is through this that they see the forms and movements of the heavenly host. However, there is neither screen nor shade between the people of heaven and the saints. Rather, they are visible and present opposite them always. There is a fiery circle surrounding the land, yet all pass in and out without its harming them. The twelve apostles and the Virgin Mary are in a special group beside the powerful Lord. Patriarchs, prophets, and the disciples of Jesus are near the apostles. There are other virgins on Mary's right, with a short distance between them. There are infants and children around them in every direction, and the song of the heavenly birds makes music for them. Radiant bands of guardian angels of the souls continually serve and minister among those companies in the presence of the King.

7   Nobody in this present world could describe or give a true account of those companies. The groups and assemblies in the aforementioned Land of the Saints, will remain in that great glory until the major assembly of Doomsday, when the just judge on the day of judgement will arrange them in the positions and places in which they are to reside, looking on the countenance of God with neither screen nor shadow between them through all eternity.

8   Though great and wonderful the splendour and brightness in the Land of the Saints, as we have related, a thousand times greater is the splendour of the Plain of the Heavenly Host, by the throne of the Lord himself. Thus is the throne, a chair fashioned with four columns of precious stones under it. If a person had no other entertainment but the harmonious music of those four columns, that in itself would give him his fill of exaltation and pleasure. There are three marvellous birds on the throne in the King's presence, and their task is to direct their attention always on the Creator. In praise and glorification of the Lord they sing the eight canonical hours, accompanied by the choir-singing of archangels. The music is begun by the birds and the archangels, and all the heavenly host, both saints and holy virgins, make the response to them.

9   Above the head of the Supreme One on his regal chair there is a huge arch, like an ornamented helmet or a royal diadem. If human eyes were to look at it they would immediately dissolve. There are three bands all around, separating these from the crowd, and no description could make known their nature. There are six thousand creatures in the form of horses and birds around the fiery chair, glowing without cease.

10   Nobody could give an account of the mighty Lord on his throne, unless he himself should do it, or unless he were to ask the heavenly orders. For no one would describe his ardour and force, his intensity and luminosity, his splendour and delightfulness, his constancy and steadfastness, the multitude of his angels and archangels making music for him, his numerous messengers coming and going to each host in turn with pleasurable utterances, his gentleness and great kindness to some, his severity and great harshness to others.

11   If a person were to look constantly about him, eastward and westward, to the south and to the north, in every direction he would find a wonderful face, seven times as bright as the sun. Yet, human form could not be perceived on it at all. Rather, it is a fiery mass blazing throughout the place, and everyone is in fear and trembling before it. Its light completely fills heaven and earth, and a ray of light like that of a majestic star surrounds it. There are three thousand different melodies for each choir singing round about it. Every single one of

their melodies are as sweet as the manifold melodies of the world.

12 Thus is the city on which is the royal seat, surrounded by seven multicoloured walls of glass. Each wall is higher than the next. The ground level and lowermost foundation of the city are of bright crystal, sun-like in appearance, with variegation of blue, crimson, green, and every colour besides.

13 The inhabitants of that city are a mild, very gentle and kindly people, without deficiency in any virtue. For none ever reach and inhabit it except holy virgins and pilgrims zealous for God. It is difficult to discover how its order and arrangement was brought about, for none of them has his back or his side towards another. Thus the ineffable power of the Lord has ordered and maintained them face to face in their ranks and circles of equal height, round about the royal throne in splendour and delight, with all their faces turned towards God.

14 Between every two choirs is a chancel-screen of crystal, with splendid ornamentation of gold and silver on it. There are outstanding rows of precious stones on those chancel-screens, variegated with different gems and with settings and circles of carbuncle. Between every two chief assemblies are three precious stones, pleasant-sounding with sweet music, and their upper halves lit up like lamps. Seven thousand angels in the form of great candles illuminate and make bright the surrounding city. Another seven thousand are in the exact centre, shedding light eternally around the royal city. If all the men of the world were in one place, however numerous they might be, the fragrance of a single one of those candles would suffice them as sustenance.

15 Those of the earthly inhabitants who do not attain that city directly at the end of their lives, and to whom their habitation is assigned after the Last Judgement, live, until Doomsday comes, in an unsettled and restless manner on heights and hills, and in marshes and uninhabited boglands. As for these hosts and assemblies, every single soul among them has its guardian angel serving and attending it.

16 At the chief entrance to the city is a screen of fire and a screen of ice, which strike against each other, end to end, throughout eternity. The

sound and din of those screens encountering each other is heard all through the world. If the descendants of Adam should hear that noise they would be seized with insupportable trembling and fear as a result. The sinners are made sad and confused by that noise. The people of heaven for their part, however, hear very little at all of the harsh sound, and it appears to them as melodious as all music.

17   Stupendous and marvellous is the narrative of the arrangement of that city, for what we have related of its various orders and wonders is but a little of a vast amount.

18   It is desolate for the soul, after its association and cohabitation with the body, in repose and ease, freedom and happiness, to set out and go to the throne of the Creator unless it goes with the guidance of angels, for it is difficult to ascend the seven heavens. No one of them is easier than another, for there are six protective gates confronting humans before they reach the heavenly kingdom. A door-keeper and guardian from the heavenly host has been assigned to keep watch at each gate.

19   At the gate of the nearest heaven is placed the archangel Michael accompanied by two virgins with iron rods in their laps to flog and beat sinners, so that it is there, then, that sinners encounter the first anguish and torment along the way on which they are travelling.

20   At the gate of the second heaven the archangel Ariel is guardian, accompanied by two virgins with fiery scourges in their hands, with which they lash sinners across their faces and eyes. A stream of fire with a great blaze on top is in front of that gate. Abersetus is the name of the angel tending that stream, who tests souls and washes from them the amount of sin which adheres to them, until they become as clean and bright as the radiance of stars. A pleasant well is situated there, and its mildness and fragrance cleans and refreshes the souls of the just. However, it tortures and burns the souls of sinners, and remits nothing from them, but rather they receive further pain and affliction there. Sinners then rise up from there in sadness and great grief. The just, however, go with happiness and gladness to the gate of the third heaven.

21   There is a fiery furnace continually burning there. Its flames rise up to

a height of twelve thousand cubits. The souls of the just go through that furnace in the twinkling of an eye. However, it sears and burns the souls of sinners for twelve years, and after that the accompanying angel takes them to the fourth gate.

22   The entrance gate of the fourth heaven is surrounded by a fiery stream like the stream already mentioned. A burning wall encircles it, with its flame measurable as twelve thousand cubits in width. The souls of the just step across it as if it were not there at all. But it detains the souls of sinners for a period of twelve years in misery and torture, until the accompanying angel conducts them to the entrance to the fifth heaven.

23   There is a further stream of fire there, but it is different from the others because there is a distinctive whirlpool in the middle of this one. This swirls around the souls of sinners, and holds them fast for sixteen years. Yet the just are able to get over it straight away, without any delay. When it is time to release the sinners, the angel strikes the stream with a rod which is hard like a stone, and lifts up the souls with the end of the rod. Then Michael takes the souls to the entrance of the sixth heaven.

24   No pain or torture is assigned to souls at that entrance, but it is lit up with the brightness and radiance of precious stones. Michael then meets up with the angel of the Trinity, and the two of them together set forth the soul before the presence of God.

25   Enormous and immeasurable then is the welcome of the inhabitants of heaven, and of the Lord himself, for the soul, if it be sinless and just. If, however, it be an unrighteous and unseemly soul, it is faced with severity and harshness from the mighty Lord, who says to the angels of heaven: "Seize this impious soul, O heavenly angels, and deliver it into the grasp of Lucifer to be submerged and stifled in the depths of hell forever". Thereupon the wretched soul is parted in a terrible, inclement manner from presence in the kingdom of heaven, and from the sight of God. Then it heaves a sigh more grievous than any other as it goes to face the devil after having seen the bliss of the kingdom of heaven. At this point it is separated from the protection of the archangels who accompanied it to heaven. Thereupon, one after another, the twelve fiery dragons suck in each soul, until the lower-

most dragon puts it into the maw of the devil. Then it suffers the entirety of every evil in the presence of the devil everlastingly.

26   When the accompanying angel had revealed to the soul of Adomnán this vision of the kingdom of heaven, and of the initial fate of each soul after its departure from the body,   the angel thereafter took Adomnán's soul to the depths of hell, with the immensity of its pains, punishments, and tortures.

27   The first land which it reached was a black burnt land, empty and scorched, where there was no punishment at all. On the far side of it was a valley full of fire. Huge flames extended past its boundaries in every direction. Its lower part was black, its middle and upper part were red. There were eight beasts there, with eyes like fiery coals. Across the valley was an enormous bridge, extending from one side to the other. It was high in the middle, but lower at its two extremities.

28   Three companies endeavour to cross it, and not all succeed. For one group, the bridge is broad from beginning to end, so that they cross the fiery chasm in complete safety, without fear or anxiety. Another group who attempt it find it narrow at first, but broad at the end, so that they thus eventually get across the chasm after great peril. For the final group, the bridge is broad at the start, but narrow and confined towards the end, so that they fall from the middle into the same terrible chasm, into the gullets of the eight raging beasts who dwell in the valley.

29   Those for whom that path was easy are the pure, those who do assiduous penitence, and those who suffered martyrdom willingly for God. The group for whom the way was narrow at first, but broad at the end are those who are compelled under duress to do the will of God, but who convert their involuntary service to willingness to serve God. Those, however, for whom the bridge was broad at first and narrow at the end are the sinners who listen to the preaching of the word of God, but who do not observe it after having heard it.

30   There are vast hosts in distress on the shore of everlasting pain opposite the land of darkness. Every second hour the pain ebbs from them. The next hour it comes over them. Those who are in this

situation are the people in whom good and evil are equally balanced. And on the Day of Judgement an appraisal will be made, and their goodness will overwhelm their evil on that day, and they will be brought thereafter to the abode of life, in the presence of God forever.

31   Near those people is another large group in terrible pain. These are bound to fiery columns, with a sea of fire around them up to their chins, and burning chains in the form of serpents around their waists. Their faces are ablaze with the pain. Those who are in such torment are sinners, those who have slain their kin, destroyers of the Church of God, and merciless ecclesiastical leaders who rule over shrines of the saints to gain the donations and tithes of the Church, making this treasure their own particular property rather than that of the invited and needy ones of the Lord.

32   There are large crowds standing continually in dank pools up to their belts. Short icy cloaks are around them. Never do the belts stop or cease from scalding them with both cold and heat. Surrounding them is a host of demons with fiery clubs, beating them about the head, and continually threatening them. The countenances of the wretched ones are all turned northward, with a harsh sharp wind directly on their faces, along with every other evil. Red showers of fire rain down on them every night and every day, and they cannot avoid them, but must eternally suffer them with weeping and lamentation.

33   Some among them have streams of fire in the hollows of their faces, some have fiery spikes through their tongues, others through their heads from outside. Those who are in that torture are thieves, deceivers, those who are treacherous and slanderous, plunderers and despoilers, judges who give false judgement, contentious people, female sorcerers and satirists, habitual bandits, and learned men who preach heresy.

34   There is another large group on islands in the middle of the sea of fire. A wall of silver surrounds them, formed from their clothing and their alms. There are people who perform acts of mercy without fail, yet who persist in slothfulness and bodily lust up to the time of their deaths. Their alms-giving renders them assistance in the midst of the fiery sea until Doomsday, and after the Judgement they are sent to the

shore of life.

35 A further great crowd there wear red fiery cloaks reaching to the ground. Their shuddering and cries are heard throughout the firmament. An innumerable host of demons stifles them, urging their accompanying stinking barbarous hounds to devour and consume them. Around the necks of these souls are red fiery discs, perpetually alight. Every second hour they are raised up to the heavens, the following hour they are cast down to the depths of hell. Those who suffer that punishment are ecclesiastics who transgress their holy orders, hypocrites, liars who deceive and lead astray the multitudes, and undertake to perform for them wonders and miracles which they are incapable of performing. It is the young, indeed, whom those in orders maim, the young who were entrusted to them to be reformed, and they did not reform them, nor did they rebuke them for their sins.

36 Yet another large group are unceasingly to and fro across the fiery flagstones, battling with the demonic hosts. Too numerous to reckon are the showers of burning-red arrows from the demons on them. They run headlong without respite or rest until they reach dark pools and rivers in order to quench the arrows in them. Plaintive and pitiful are the cries and wails uttered by the sinners in those waters, for it is an increase of pain which is in store for them. Those who endure such torture are dishonest craftsmen, comb-makers, and merchants, false-adjudicating judges, both among the Jews and among all others, impious kings, iniquitious and sinful religious superiors, adulterous women, and the messengers who seduce them into their misdeeds.

37 There is a wall of fire opposite the land of punishments. This is seven times more terrible and fierce than the land of punishments itself. However, no soul ever dwells there, for it is solely in the care of demons until the Day of Judgement.

38 Woe to whoever is in the foregoing torments in the company of the devil's host. Woe to the one who does not beware of that host. Woe to him whose lord is a fierce disparaging demon. Woe to the one who listens to the cries and weeping of the souls bewailing and lamenting to the Lord that Judgement-Day should come speedily so that they might find out if they were to receive any alleviation thereby, for they

never get any respite except for three hours every Sunday. Woe to the person for whom that land is his assigned habitation forever. For this, indeed, is how it is, empty thorny mountains there, bare burnt plains, and foul verminous lakes. It is a rough, sand-covered land, rugged and frozen, with broad fiery slabs in its midst, and great seas with fierce storms. In it is the abode and dwelling of the devil for eternity. Through the middle of it run four great rivers, a river of fire, a river of snow, a river of poison, and a river of dark black water. In these the savage demonic hosts bathe, after their sport and diversion in torturing the souls.

39 When the blessed hosts of the heavenly household sing the harmonious melodies of the eight canonical hours praising the Lord joyfully and gladly, it is then that the souls utter pitiful sorrowful laments, as they are being beaten without cease by the throngs of demons.

40 These, then, are the tortures and punishments which the accompanying angel revealed to the soul of Adomnán after its visit to the kingdom of heaven. In the twinkling of an eye, the soul was brought through the golden porch and through the crystal screen to the Land of the Saints, where it had first been brought when it went forth from the body. When it became desirous of staying and residing in that land it heard from behind, through the screen, the voice of the angel commanding it to go back to the same body from which it had emerged, so that in assemblies and gatherings, and at meetings of layfolk and clerics, Adomnán might relate the rewards of heaven and the pains of hell, just as the accompanying angel had revealed to him.

41 Thereafter, this was the teaching which Adomnán always used to preach to the crowds for as long as he lived. It was what he taught at the great assembly of the men of Ireland when the Law of Adomnán was imposed on the Irish, and the women were rendered free by Finnachta Fledach, king of Ireland, and by the nobles of Ireland as well. Moreover, the rewards of heaven and the punishments of hell were the first tidings which Patrick son of Calpurnius used to relate to those who believed in the Lord through his teaching, and who accepted his spiritual direction by embracing the gospel.

42 The teaching most frequently proclaimed by Peter and Paul and the

other apostles also concerned these punishments and rewards, for they had been revealed to them in a similar manner. It was that teaching which Silvester, abbot of Rome, preached to Constantine son of Helena, High-King of the world, at the assembly in which he offered Rome to Peter and Paul. It was the same which Fabian, the successor of Peter, preached to Philip son of Gordian, king of the Romans, through which he believed in the Lord, and many thousand others believed at that time. He, indeed, was the first king of the Romans who believed in the Lord Jesus Christ.

43   These were also the tidings which Elijah relates to the souls of the just while beneath the tree of life in Paradise. Once Elijah opens the book to teach the souls, the spirits of the just come to him from every direction in the form of radiant birds. He tells them first of the rewards of the just, the delight and pleasures of the kingdom of heaven. That much makes them joyful. However, he then tells them of the punishments and tortures of hell, and the terrors of Doomsday. And a look of sorrow is clearly manifested on him and on Enoch, so that they are thus the two sorrows of the kingdom of heaven. Then Elijah shuts the book, and thereupon the birds emit a great cry of lamentation, and they press their wings close to their bodies until streams of blood flow from them, in their fear of the punishment of hell and the Day of Judgement.

44   Since the souls of the blessed, who are assigned an everlasting dwelling in the kingdom of heaven, lament in this manner, so should the people of the world fittingly shed tears of blood as they take heed of Doomsday and the punishment of hell. For then the Lord will render to everyone in the world his due, giving rewards to the just, and punishments to sinners. Thereafter the souls will be placed in the depths of everlasting pain, and by the word of God they will be enclosed, by the malediction of the judge of Doomsday, for all eternity. The blessed and the just, the alms-givers and the merciful, will be borne to the right hand of God, to live forever in the kingdom of heaven, where they will be in great glory, without age or withering, without end or termination forever.

45   Thus is that city, a kingdom without pride or arrogance, without falsehood or deception, without deprivation or penitence, without

hostility or encounter, without shame or disgrace. without envy or haughtiness, without pestilence or disease, without poverty or nakedness, without damage or destruction, without hail-showers or snow, without wind or rain, without din or thunder, without darkness or coldness. It is a noble, splendid, delightful kingdom, fruitful and bright, with the fragrance of a faultless land in which every excellence is enjoyed.

27. ANTICHRIST

1   The Lord said that Antichrist would be the devil who would come in human form, and that he would perform great signs among the people. He would say that he was the true son of God, the one who had always been prophesied, and that no one should presume to assert that Christ had come before him to succour the human race. John the Evangelist said to Jesus: "O Lord, in what manner will that man appear? We should have a written description, so that he may be recognized by his evil deeds, so that, thus recognized, allegiance would not be given him".

2   The Lord said that he would be born in Bethlehem, of a harlot of the tribe of Daniel, that he would be reared in the Carbuban (*sic*), and that he would live in the city called Besasta. His body will be six hundred lengths high, and forty in width. He will have a single eye protruding from his forehead, with a flat-surfaced face, and a mouth extending as far as his chest. He will have no upper teeth, nor will he have knees, and the soles of his feet will be rounded like a cart-wheel. He will have fearsome black hair, and three fiery vapours from his nose and mouth which will rise in the air like flames of fire.

3   Nobody in the world will be able to hide himself from him. With red-hot iron he will brand a mark on the forehead of every person who believes in him, and no one in the world can ever conceal that mark even till Doomsday. He will kill all who will not believe in him, and these will be among God's elect. He will raise the dead in imitation of Christ, with sinners being the ones who are raised thus. He will tear trees up by the roots, setting the roots uppermost, and causing the fruit to come up through the roots, by the powers of the devil.

4   In that man's time, rivers will turn and face up heights. Father will kill son, and son father. Kinsman will kill kinsman, and there will be neither faith nor honour at that time. Churches will be destroyed, and priests will flee, unmindful of the relics of the saints who had preceded

them, or of the churches where the saints had dwelt. The women serving in church will be without modesty, flaunting their shame and nakedness.

5   On the day of the birth of Antichrist, there will be someone dead in every house throughout the four corners of the world. Later on, the two prophets now in Paradise, Elijah and Enoch, will come to do battle with him. They will fight together for three hundred and forty days, and thereafter he will slay them both in the Plati, that is, in the palace of the city of Jerusalem. They will lie dead for three and a half days, during which time nobody will dare to bury them for fear of Anti-christ. Then, at midday, they will arise in the presence of all. And an angel will descend from heaven, and will say to them: "O Elijah and Enoch, enter into eternal life from henceforth". And they will ascend then in the sight of all the people.

6   Then there will be an earthquake and terrible fiery thunder upon the hosts. Everyone in the company of Antichrist will be burnt and killed by the power of God. Thereafter, to save the people, almighty God will send the archangel Michael, carrying a naked sword. He will slay Antichrist with a single blow, splitting him in two halves from the crown of his head down to the ground. Michael did not deliver that blow simply to destroy Antichrist, but to return the world to a better state. Then every pagan, Jew, and foreigner will convert to the Catholic faith. Only three and a half years will remain after that until the Day of Judgement.

28. THE SEVEN JOURNEYS OF THE SOUL

1   The first day's journey of the soul - harsh its tribulation - is to noble Jerusalem, where Jesus suffered.

2   On the following day, the course which it travels, according to procedure, is to the beautiful river Jordan, where it was redeemed through baptism.

3   On the third day, this is the glorious course of every soul without disgrace, that it may see the happiness of the Paradise of Adam which had been abandoned.

4   The fourth saving journey - it is not an advance into confusion - is to the royal kingdom, the loyal force of angels with God.

5   After that, on the fifth day, it reaches very cold and terrible hell - not a peaceful and gentle place - where demons are tortured.

6   On the sixth bright day - better if it be a step without shame - it travels back to its body again, whether it be evil or good that it will do.

7   The seventh day of the great journey - perhaps it is a step toward its battlefield - that is the day on which it is conveyed to hell or heaven.

8   It would be better for every Christian, even though he should devote himself to good work, to weep with copious tears on the first day of his departure from the world.

9   It is Moelmoedóc son of Diarmaid who bestows the abundant knowledge as far as heaven of bright paths. It is he who sang the song.

28A. PROSE TEXT

The soul makes seven journeys after it leaves the body. They are as follows: on the first day to the city of Jerusalem, on the second day to Bethlehem, on the third day to Paradise, on the fourth day to heaven, on the fifth day to the river Jordan, on the sixth day, back to the same body again, on the seventh day, the consignment of the soul to heaven or hell or some other place.

29. THE SIGNS BEFORE DOOMSDAY

1 Every Christian, even one who sheds tears every canonical hour, should fear the calamitous Sunday of the week before the Day of Judgement.

2 There will be a mighty sound and horrible harsh cries on that last Sunday before the resurrection of the dead.

3 A red fiery cloud will come from the northerly part of the heavens. It will be ugly, harsh, fierce and fearful as it spreads over the earth.

4 A blood-filled rain will fall from the dark gloomy cloud. It will fill the whole world - a woeful change for our peoples.

5 At the third hour, penetrating fearful showers of blood will begin. They will be numerous, and will not go away until Sunday midday.

6 There will be blazing lightning, and unwelcome thunder, harsh hail-showers, and showers of blood.

7 From midday until nones - it is not to be concealed- there will be an enfolding bloody rain throughout the four quarters of the world.

8 There will be eruptions of the earth, horrible noisy quaking, and the sea with its animals overflowing its great ramparts.

9 Woe to everyone who does not pay attention in time. It is proper for us to have due fear of the Judgement.

10 On the second day, hosts will be distressed. No regions of pleasure will exist. The heavens will tremble around the earth.

11 Waves of sea-water will come up to the high coast-lands. Sea-monsters will roar, and will utter fierce sounds.

12   There will be terrible lamenting and crying, and unmelodious wailing. Throughout the four corners of the world there will be intense agitation, without peace, without direction.

13   Existence will be sorrowful, lacking in peace and full joy. The elect, with good works, will be in privation on dark shores.

14   As for the wretched bitter peoples, robbers will strike them with fists. It is not a sleep of pleasant peace which pervades. Flames will fill the hillsides.

15   Let each one cry out to God - what protection is swifter - that our Lord of bright generosity will save us on that day.

16   On the third bright day, on Tuesday, the ramparts [of the world] strike against each other, when our just fair Lord leans on the globe of his creation.

17   The deep foundations of the world will crumble - a sure matter. Splendidly-shaped stones will shake. Their appearance will be destroyed.

18   Red fiery clouds, which are sharp, cutting, and merciless, will circle around the world. It will not be a pleasant, easy, agreeable course.

19   A stream of sulphurous fire will come forth from the corners of the many-sided earth, in such a way that it will cause trembling on the surface of the wet world.

20   There will be a single, ever-curving flame from east to west. An evil treacherous mist will fill every extremity as far as the reddening sea.

21   May the King of ample prosperity who created the rays of the sun protect us with his hosts of archangels on the third day.

22   On the fourth ominous day of Wednesday, with hundreds of fears, there will come an outburst of lamentation which will shake the whole world.

23   The great-waved sea will rise up from the earth in floods. Its mighty roar will reach as far as the clouds of heaven.

24   There will be the clamour of the bellowing sea-monsters and of the red-mouthed spiky beasts, and of the hosts of creatures with snorting gills on the dry shore.

25   The great sea will sink down again with enormous tumult, so that its course is unknown, as it submerges under the surface of the earth.

26   A pacifying calm then comes into the view of the hosts, bringing restoration again, so that it returns within its proper boundaries.

27   There are fierce sharp voracious winds with hundreds of breezes, which smash the woodlands, and carry them off into the air.

28   Wicked noisy bird-flocks circle around every great land. Swiftly, firmly, and intently, they swoop down on the food of the land.

29   Wondrous signs will appear, harsh hail-showers with terrible blood. The descendants of Adam are chastized. Wretched are their circumstances in every place.

30   The sorrowful host of the race of Adam in their ranks will utter the exhausted sorrowful remark: "Better for us to be dead than alive".

31   There will be continual raging uproar, fearful ferocious vibrations. Streaming torrents will separate from the sea.

32   The famed heavens will be turned around to their very depths. Their usual course will be upset, as they smash against the earth.

33   May the great Son of the Virgin Mary save us with his outstanding goodness from every ensnaring evil on the fourth ominous day.

34   On the fifth illustrious day, on Thursday, avenging thunderstorms will come with much fire. The stars of heaven will be thrown down.

35   It is evident that every outstanding created thing is beaten down and

wretched. The firm stable world has lost its enduring steadfastness.

36   Sorrows will be deep, and horrors will be vast. Swift supernatural streams will fill the space from heaven to earth.

37   Multitudes of stars will fall down from their firm positions. They cannot show forth their light. The sun and moon will be extinguished.

38   There will be fearful wailing and lamenting, extreme gloom and sadness, with no guidance or direction, no peace or bright gladness.

39   There will be disagreeable streams hidden beneath hail-showers. They will be gloomy, rapid, and undulating amidst the flames of fire.

40   The divine God who has chosen me, who readily watches over hosts, may he save me, along with all the saints, from the events of the fifth day.

41   On the sixth full day, on Friday, the great martyrdom will be inflicted on all the race of Adam.

42   Wise men will not conceal it. They relate clearly in order that every creature that ever lived will die a sudden death.

43   It will be a sorrowful carnage beneath the hailstones. It will not be noisy, busy, filled with steeds along the flaming hillsides.

44   The beautiful gates of splendid faultless heaven will be opened. The hosts of heaven with wonderful brightness will cover the world.

45   The saints and holy angels in the broad swift light, in every way as free as fish in the sea.

46   After assuming earthly bodies, at the right hand of holy Christ they will assuredly live in perpetual union. Fortunate the one who attains it.

47   On the Saturday of the week, the world will tremble. It will pour forth a tumult of harsh vapour like a boiling cauldron.

48 It will emit its terrible showers angrily from its vapours. Swift flames will disturb hillsides. They will extend upwards over the mountains.

49 Bitter streams will dry up in ghostly rows, being without flood or wave, without majestically-arranged currents.

50 The ridges of the smooth mountains will be threateningly divided. They will be balefully destroyed. They will be shattered fiercely.

51 The essence of every element will change - a remarkable report. They will change so that they will not be dwelling-places either for the living or the dead.

52 The High-King of the kingdom of heaven, Holy Christ who rules every assembly, may our leader protect us, and may he save us on the Saturday.

53 On the day of the completion, on Sunday, an apparition to us in our troubles, the hosts of archangels will come to earth with our Lord.

54 The archangel will utter a clear call over the body of every person of the race of noble Adam, summoning all to rise.

55 The first resurrection at the call of the archangel, before everyone, is that of the apostles, going with tumult to Christ without difficulty.

56 In the second resurrection the prophets of the world will arise. In the third clamorous awakening will be confessors.

57 In the fourth resurrection the martyrs of the earth will arise. In the fifth resurrection, the host of the saints in its entirety.

58 In the sixth resurrection there will arise from their earthly lodging the chaste and the penitents, and infants who have been baptized.

59 In the seventh resurrection everyone with a soul will arise from fire, from great floods, from sea and land and earth.

60 The huge company will come together in fear for an assembly, the holy

host of heaven, the people of earth, and the host of hell.

61 It is a steadfast assembly, with those who are valued and beloved arranged and ranked in front of the bright countenance of the King of the seven heavens.

62 The noble seven heavens will be turned about...A fierce fire will advance from east to west.

63 At the edges of that flame will be the array of the host in rows, above the triumphant lightning, awaiting the judgements of Doomsday.

64 The outstanding king will rise, so that he is visible to all, with his red oppressive cross on his back in the sight of all.

65 The fearless Son of God the Father will sit in his seat of glory. with the twelve apostles around him in a brilliant company.

66 O Son of the Hebrew Virgin, who created great hosts, shelter our conspicuous misery, to protect us on that day.

67 On the Sunday of the assembly, after the frantic resurrection, the black host of demons will come - it will not be a pleasant noble happening.

68 The multitudes of the host of hell, unredeemed in their prisons, will fill the whole world with the harshness of their ferocity.

69 The idols, dark gods of sinful heathens, will fall. Their deeds cannot survive being in the presence of the High-King.

70 There will be vast amounts of red flame, a red fire which consumes valuables, terrible tribulations, with much anger before them.

71 The deep foundations of the world will stir - a sorrowful circumstance. It will lapse into unsubstantial silence, without advantage, strength...

72 There will be awful crying and bawling, unceasing, immoderate, without gentleness, comfort or peace, opposite the bright ranks.

73 There are mysterious twisting streams which over-run the edge of the flame. People loathe the dark active trembling above the hail.

74 Let us pray to the great Lord at every hour to save us from our wretched troubles on the Sunday of the assembly.

75 On the bright Monday of Judgement, for which punishments amass, the angelic hosts will wage battle against the fierce demons.

76 The vile host without difficulty will be subdued in its frenzy, with much lamentation, by the angels. The dark demons will be defeated.

77 They will be cast back weeping to hell with their fraudulent leader Lucifer, harsher than a lion.

78 Thereafter, true judgements will be delivered on the descendants of Adam in the sight of God. They will be divided according to their deeds. They will be set apart in groups.

79 Sinners without generosity will be banished with the demonic host into the cold pains of hell, to tremble in severe gloom.

80 Every righteous person will be at the right hand of God everlastingly. Every lawless person will be set at his left hand, and destined for hell.

ABBREVIATIONS, MANUSCRIPTS, JOURNALS

Atkinson, *Passions and Homilies*, R. Atkinson, *The Passions and Homilies from Leabhar Breac* (Todd Lecture Series 2), Dublin:Royal Irish Academy, 1887.

BL: The British Library (formerly, The British Museum), London.

Book of Leinster: MS, Trinity College, Dublin, H 2 18; diplomatic text R. I. Best, O. Bergin, M. A. O'Brien, A. O'Sullivan, *The Book of Leinster formerly Lebar na Núachongbála*, vols 1-6, Dublin Institute for Advanced Studies, 1954-1983.

Book of Uí Maine: MS, Royal Irish Academy, D ii 1; see R. A. S. Macalister, *The Book of Uí Maine otherwise called "The Book of the O'Kelly's"*, Dublin, 1942.

CMCS: Cambridge Medieval Celtic Studies. Published at the Department of Anglo-Saxon, Norse and Celtic, University of Cambridge .

Celtica: Journal, published by the Dublin Institute for Advanced Studies.

Éigse: Journal, published by the National University of Ireland.

Ériu: Journal, published by the Royal Irish Academy, Dublin.

Études Celtiques: Journal; Paris.

Irish Theological Quarterly: Journal; St. Patricks College, Maynooth.

JThS: Journal of Theological Studies.

Leabhar Breac: MS 23 P 16 Royal Irish Academy, Dublin; published in facs. by RIA, 1876; Passions and Homilies from, ed. R. Atkinson.

Lebor Gabála Érenn. The Book of the Taking of Ireland, ed. R. A. S. Mac-Alister, parts I-V (Irish Texts Society 34, 35,39, 41,44*)*, Dublin, 1938-1956.

Lebor na hUidre: MS 23 E 25, Royal Irish Academy, Dublin;ed. R. I. Best and O. J. Bergin, *Lebor na hUidre: Book of the Dun Cow*, Dublin: Royal Irish Academy, 1929.

Liber Flavus Fergusiorum: MS, 23 O 48, vol. i, ii, Royal Irish Academy, Dublin.

Milltown Studies: Journal, published by the Milltown Institute of Theology and Philiosophy, Dublin.

McNamara: Martin McNamara, *The Apocrypha in the Irish Church*, Dublin Institute for Advanced Studies, 1975; reprint, with corrections 1984.

NLI: National Library of Ireland, Dublin.

Peritia: Journal of the Medieval Academy of Ireland, Cork and Galway.

PRIA: Proceedings of the Royal Irish Academy, Dublin.

Revue Celtique: Journal, Paris; succeeded by *Études Celtiques.*

RIA: Royal Irish Academy, Dublin.

Studia Celtica: Journal, published on behalf of the Board of Celtic Studies of the University of Wales.

Yellow Book of Lecan: MS, Trinity College, Dublin, H 2 16. Facsimile. Introduction by R. Atkinson, Dublin 1896.

ZCP: Zeitschrift für celtische Philologie, Journal, published by Niemeyer, Tübingen.

1. THE CREATION OF ADAM

Text of British Library MS Egerton 1782, f 45.

There are a number of traditions, both Christian and Jewish, on the creation of Adam, and also on his burial. The two latter often correspond to one another, the burial place being that of the creation. These traditions, originally apparently distinct, tended to become combined. Most of the Christian traditions were probably originally Jewish, or are based on Jewish material, which has been adapted to the Christian context. The traditions often originated in a theological consideration regarding the place of Adam, the first man, or of Adam and Eve the first pair, in the overall plan of creation. Adam was, in a sense, universal man, a truth written into the accounts of his creation.

One preoccupation was to see the universal nature of Adam in his name, or in the clay or elements from which he was created. The four letters that compose his name were seen as derived from the initials of the Greek words for the cardinal points *Anatole, Dysis, Arctos, Mesembria* (East, West, North, South). This tradition is extremely common in Patristic and Medieval texts. While it seems to have been ultimately based on 2 (or Slavonic) Enoch 30,13 ("And I assigned to him [i.e. man] a name from the four components: from East, from West, from North, from South"), transmitted in Slavonic from what appears a Greek original, its use in the West may have been through Augustine; see R. McNally, *Der irische Liber de Numeris*, Munich, 1957, 72f. It is found in text no. 2, par. 3 of this collection, combined with another to be mentioned below.

There was a tradition that he was created from clay taken from the centre of the world, from Jerusalem, Mount Moriah, the mount of sacrifice (of Isaac, the temple sacrifices) and site of the future temple and that he was buried there. This tradition was Christianised, with Calvary (the place of Christ's sacrifice) replacing the site of the temple. See L. Ginzberg, *The Legends of the Jews*, Philadelphia, 1909 (reprint 1968),I, 55, 101; V, notes 16 (p. 73), 167 (pp. 125-127).

Other traditions are that he was created from earth from Hebron; that, with Abraham, Isaac and Jacob, he was buried in Hebron, earlier called Kiryath-Arba, "the City of the Four (Men)". This Jewish tradition is recorded by Jerome (*Hebraicae quaestiones in Genesim* 23,2 (CCL 72, 28). This is sometimes combined with the preceding one by having Adam's body transported to Jerusalem (by the Flood, for instance) where it is buried. See text 4, par. 50-53.

A belief widespread in tradition, Irish included, is the formation of Adam's body from sods from different parts of the world. It is found in text no. 2, par. 3 of this collection, combined with another on derivation of the name Adam. See David Wassserstein, "The Creation of Adam and the Apocrypha in Early Ireland", *PRIA* 88 C(1988), 1-17.

A further tradition still is formation of Adam from eight *pondera*; see M.McNamara, *The Apocrypha*, p. 22f.

The tradition of par. 2-3 of this present text on the creation of Adam, of man, from seven components is more rarely found. It is very similar to the section of 2 Enoch (30, 8) which immediately precedes that on the derivation of Adam's name, and may well derive from it. The text of 2 Enoch reads:

> And on the sixth day I commanded my wisdom to create man out of the seven components: [1] his flesh from earth; [second] his blood from dew and from the sun; [third] his eyes from the bottomless sea (a variant has his eyes from the sun); [fourth] his bones from stone; [fifth] his reason from the mobility of angels and from clouds; [sixth] his veins and hair from the grass of the earth; [seventh] his spirit from my spirit and from wind.
> (translation by F. I. Andersen in *The Old Testament Pseudepigrapha*, J. H. Charlesworth, ed., I, London, 1983, 150.)

2. CREATION AND FALL

McNamara no. 1Ba;

Text of *Leabhar Breac*, beginning 109bi, collated with text of RIA MS 23 O 48 (*Liber Flavus*), ii, 21ra. Originally edited by B. McCarthy, *The Codex Palatino-Vaticanus No. 830* (Todd Lecture Series 3, Dublin, 1892), 45-59.

This is a prose version of Cantos IV through IX of *Saltair na Rann*, lines 833-1436 of the editions (cf. edition by Whitley Stokes, *Saltair na Rann*, Anecdota Oxoniensia. Medieval and Modern Series, I, iii, Oxford, 1883). It follows the verse original fairly faithfully, but has some additions and paraphrases from the larger Adam and Eve tradition that can be presumed to have been current. Thus in par. 3 it gives the vernacular equivalents for the Greek names for the cardinal points and adds the further tradition on the four sods from which Adam was made (on this see introduction to no. 1). In the same place it makes explicit mention of the mountains of Pariath, a geographical detail of Paradise found in other Irish texts as well.

The sources of *Saltair na Rann* have been examined in detail by St. J. D. Seymour (*PRIA* 36 C, 1921-24, 121-133), and those for this section by Brian O. Murdoch (*The Irish Adam and Eve Story from Saltair na Rann*, II, Commentary, Dublin, 1976). The chief source is the apocryphal *Vita Adae et Evae*, with contributions from the apocryphal *Apocalypsis Mosis*. Murdoch's comments on the *Saltair* hold good for this prose paraphrase too.

3. THE PENANCE OF ADAM

McNamara no. 1Ba4;

Text of RIA MS 25 P 25, ff 64vb-65rb11, collated with versions in *Leabhar Breac* (ed. B. McCarthy, *The Codex Palatino-Vaticanus No. 830*, pp. 60-71), and the Yellow Book of Lecan, col 846-848. For another version see Alan O. Anderson, "Peannaid Adaim", *Revue Celtique* 24 (1903), 243-53.

The opening section (chaps 1-17) of the *Vita Adae et Evae* gives a decscription of the repentance of the first parents. This present text follows the *Vita* so closely that this would appear to be its main, if not its sole, source. Thus:

par. 1, *Vita* 1 (-2);

par. 2, *Vita* 3;

par. 3, *Vita* 4;

par. 4, *Vita* 5;

par. 5, *Vita* 6-7 ("Adam said to Eve,'I will spend forty days fasting, but you rise and go to the Tigris River ... and stand in the water of the river for thirty-seven days'", *Vita* 6. The Irish texts in general read "Tibir" for Tigris. In par. 5 there may be an influence from the *Apocalypsis Mosis* (29,13), not found in the *Vita*, in the angels and living creatures assembled around Adam.

par. 6 (second temptation of Eve), *Vita* 9; *Apoc. Mosis* 29, 15-16;

par. 7, *Vita* 9-10; *Apoc. Mosis* 29,15-16;

par. 8, *Vita* 11 (Eve speaks);

par. 9, *Vita* 12-13;

par. 10, *Vita* 14-15;

par. 11, *Vita* 16;

par. 12, cf. *Vita* 16;

par. 13, cf. *Vita* 17.

4. THE DEATH OF ADAM

Verse text of *Saltair na Rann*;. see David Greene and Fergus Kelly, ed., *The Irish Adam and Eve Story*, vol. I, (Dublin, 1976). lines 2021-2240.

The sources of this section of *Saltair na Rann* have been investigated in detail by Brian O. Murdoch in *The Irish Adam and Eve Story from Saltair na Rann*, vol. II, Commentary, pp. 138-147. It is the final section of the Irish Adam and Eve Book in *Saltair na Rann* and has elements both from the *Apocalypsis Mosis* and the *Vita Adae et Evae*. The poet is not following *Apocalypsis Mosis* as such - some details and the ordering are substantially different. Neither is the *Vita Adae et Evae* the source, although it is clearly demonstrable that the origins are Latin. The *Saltair* text at least presents evidence of an Adambook in Latin that preserves far more of the elements known otherwise from the *Apocalypsis Mosis* than any of the extant texts. A very interesting feature of the *Saltair* text, compared with other vernacular derivatives of the *Vita Adae et Evae tradition* in any form, is the virtual exclusion of the role of Seth (Murdoch, p. 138). This Seth tradition, however, was known in Ireland through its presence in the Gospel of Nicodemus III(XIX) (text no. 19 of the present collection).

5. ADAM AND HIS DESCENDANTS

Extracts from poem beginning *Athair caich coimsid nimi*, from the Book of Uí Maine, beginning f 94a, collated with text found in several recensions of *Lebor Gabála*, published by R.A.S. MacAllister, *Lebor Gabála Érenn*, Part 1 (Dublin, 1938), 172-97.

This text was probably composed from a variety of traditions and sources. Some Irish elements appear, e.g. the Mount of Partech (par. 1) and the well of Partiach (par. 2) in Paradise. Note also Cain's murder of Abel with the jaw-bone of a camel. It remains for future research to identify the sources of the other traditions.

6. THE TWO SORROWS OF THE KINGDOM
OF HEAVEN

McNamara no. 9;

Text of *Lebor na hUidre*, ff 17-18 (diplomatic edition, ed. R.I. Best and O. Bergin, *Lebor na hUidre*, Dublin, 1929, lines 1356-1429) with omissions supplied from version in the Book of Leinster, pp 280-281.

This is an apocryphal work to which much scholarly attention has been given, although it is here being translated into English for the first time. Its points of contact with the Enoch and Elijah tradition and the Antichrist legend have been noted. M. R. James (*The Cambridge Medieval History*, vol. 3, 1922, 505) was of the opinion "that it is a document based on an *apocryphon* which it is safe to say, belongs to eastern Christendom". St John D. Seymour (*PRIA* 37 C, 1926, 110-111) has pointed out similarities between this work and other Irish compositions which speak of Enoch and Elijah preaching on the Day of Doom to souls under the form of birds.

The work may very well be composite, putting together, even juxtaposing, independent traditions on the central theme. We may note that while both Enoch and Elijah are mentioned at the beginning and the end, in the central section only Elijah features. More light will probably be cast on the nature and origin of the composition when studied against the background of the Elijah apocryphal tradition (e.g. *The Apocalypse of Elijah*), of which the Antichrist is an integral part, and of the Enoch and Elijah tradition. See Richard J. Bauckham ("The Martyrdom of Enoch and Elijah: Jewish or Christian?", *Jour. Bib. Lit.* 95, 1976, 447-478), K. Berger (*Die Auferstehung des Propheten und die Erhöhung des Menschensohnes. Traditionsgeschichtliche Untersuchungen zur Deutung des Geschickes Jesu in frühchristlichen Texten*, Studien zur Umwelt des N.T. 13, Göttingen, 1976).

Comparison of further items of the Irish text, such as the particular form of the Antichrist tradition, with analogous material in texts from Ireland and elsewhere may also help to identify more closely the work's literary associations.

This particular apocryphon seems to have been one of the sources used by author of *The Vision of Adomnán* (text 26, par. 43 of this collection).

7. STORY OF DAVID

Text from Yellow Book of Lecan, f. 121b; transcribed by Kuno Meyer, *ZCP* 13 (1920), 177.

This is a garbled account of the biblical narrative concerning Absalom, David, Uriah, Joab, Nathan, and Saul, from 1 and 2 Samuel. It begins with an account of Absalom and his growth of hair, from 2 Sam 14:25-26. It goes on to speak of the David's adultery with the wife of Uriah, and events of the second Ammonite campaign (2 Sam 11). Uriah is given as David's soldier; Joab appears as Absalom. In paragraph no. 2 "Absalom" in the first occurrence stands for Joab of 2 Sam 10, next as Joab's messenger of 2 Sam 10:22. The next part is based on Nathan's dealings with David according to 2 Sam 12, Nathan's name being replaced by "the lad". Behind the first part of the last paragraph there must stand the account of Saul's attempt on David's life (1 Sam 19:10), followed immediately by a passage apparently based on David's behaviour on the death of his child by Bathsheba (2 Sam 12:16-19).

8. THE POWER OF WOMEN

McNamara no. 10B;

Text of Book of Leinster, 282a (*Book of Leinster* vol. 5, 36554-36618)

This is a version of the famous tale on the relative strength of wine, kings and women, found also in the apocryphal work 1 (3) Esdras 3:1-4:32. (The fourth section on the strength of truth in 4:33-41 was added in the later transmission of the story; only the first three are envisaged in 3:12.). In 1(3) Esdras the king is the Persian Darius, and the first two speakers are anonymous, while the third is identified as (the Jew) Zerubbabel. The story is older than 1(3) Esdras, the author of which book adapted it for his own purposes. A variant form, differing in a number of ways from that of 1(3) Esdras, is found in Josephus, *Antiquities* 11,2,2-9.

9. THE DEATHS OF THE CHIEF PROPHETS

Text of Bodleian MS Rawlinson B 502, 75a, collated with text of *Leabhar Breac*, p. 181b. See *The Irish Sex Aetates Mundi*, ed. Dáibhí Ó Cróinín (Dublin, 1983), pp. 93, 129.

There is an apocryphal work entitled "The Lives of the Prophets", extant in a number of versions, including Syriac, Ethiopic, Latin and Armenian, but all depending on Greek originals. It begins: "The names of the prophets, and where they are from, and where they died and how, and where they lie". This includes lives of the four major, twelve minor prophets and some others (Nathan, Abijah, Joad, Azariah, Elijah, Elisha and Zechariah son of Jehoiada). The original language was probably Semitic, and was of Jewish rather than Christian origin, although this is not certain.

Material of the kind found in this apocryphon was also transmitted in non-apocryphal works, e.g. the genuine Isidorian *De ortu et obitu patrum* (PL 83, 129-175) and the pseudo-Isidorian, and probably Irish, adaptation of this: *Liber de ortu et obitu patriarcharum*. The precise origins and precedents of the Irish piece, here translated, remains to be determined. On early latin texts see also F. Dolbeau, "Deux opuscules latins, relatifs aux personnages de la Bible et antérieurs à Isidore de Seville", *Revue d'histoire des textes* 16(1986), 83-139 (on the pre-Isidorian works: the pseudo-Epiphanius, *Libellus...priorum Prophetarum*, and the *De ortu et obitu Prophetarum et Apostolorum*).

10. INFANCY GOSPEL

McNamara, nos 37, 43;

Text (with minor omissions), is that of RIA MS 23 O 48 (*Liber Flavus Fergusiorum*), ii, ff 5va-7ra. Here, as elsewhere, omissions are indicated thus: ... .

In 1895 Edmund Hogan published from the *Leabhar Breac* an Irish Infancy Narrative, under the title "Legends on the Childhood of Christ" (E. Hogan, *The Irish Nennius from L. na hUidre and Homilies and Legends from L. Breac*, Todd Lecture Series 6, Dublin, 1895). In 1927 M. R. James republished the English translation of this, together with two Latin texts (BL Arundel 404 and Hereford, MS O. 3. 9 in the Library of the Dean and Chapter) (M.R. James, *Latin Infancy Gospels*, Cambridge). In 1976 Jan Gijsel published a study of these two Latin texts, of their sources, provenance and date of origin. He argued that the Infancy Narrative of these two texts originated in south-west Germany in the Carolingian age (Jan Gijsel,"Les 'Evangiles latins de l'Enfance'de M. R. James", *Analecta Bollandiana* 94, 1976, 289-302).

The Irish text here presented in translation in the manuscript forms part of a longer work which begins with the upbringing of Mary. It provides further information for the study of Irish Infancy narratives, and especially of the recension known through the Latin texts, of which more are now known to scholars than the two edited by M. R. James.

11. THE WONDERS OF THE NIGHT OF THE NATIVITY

McNamara, no.44A;

Text of *Leabhar Breac*, 132b-133b, collated with other manuscript copies. On the text tradition, see Brian ÓCuív, "The seventeen won-

Vernam Hull. "The Middle Irish Apocryphal account of 'The seventeen miracles at Christ's birth' ", *Modern Philology* 43 (1945-6), 25-39. Additional matter on the Magi inserted into the text of the thirteenth wonder in the Leabhar Breac and related texts is printed separately as no. 13 below.

In what may be an earlier source used by the compiler, or perhaps even a later interpolation, Joseph in the *Protoevangelium Iacobi* (18,2) speaks of nature standing still and of other marvels taking place at the birth of Christ. "And I [Joseph] looked up at the vault of heaven, and saw it standing still and the birds of the heaven motionless. And I looked at the earth, and saw a dish placed there and workmen lying round it, with their hands in the dish. But those who chewed did not chew, and those who lifted up anything lifted up nothing, and those who put something to their mouth put nothing (to their mouth), but all had their faces turned upwards. And behold, sheep were being driven and (yet) they did not come forward, but stood still; and the shepherd raised his hand to strike them with his staff; but his hand remained up. And I looked at the flow of the river, and saw the mouths of kids over it and they did not drink. And then all at once everything went on its course (again)" (translation as in E.Hennecke-W. Schneemelcher, *New Testament Apocrypha*, I,383f.). The passage on the cessation of nature at Christ's birth is also in the Arundel and Hereford Infancy Gospels (par. 72), in the Irish Infancy Narrative, edited by Hogan (par. 68) and in the text no 10 above (par. 14).

It may be that the tradition found in Irish texts of the seventeen (or sixteen) wonders on the night Christ was born developed from that on the silence or cessation of nature. The precise sources behind these wonders, however, remain to be determined. Robin Flower expressed the view that the "theme" for the Irish account of the seventeen miracles was a passage of Orosius' *Historiarum adversum paganos libri VII* (6,18; ed. Zangmeister, CSEL 5, 413), where the Roman historian mentions three portents announcing the advent of Christ. Arguments in favour of this might be seen in the fact that Orosius' text is clearly used in what appear to be Hiberno-Latin commentaries on Luke (*Expositio IV Evangeliorum*, in Luke 2, PL 30, 587CD and the anonymous Vienna Commentary, *In Lucam* 2, ed. CCL 108C, 13). A stronger argument might be seen in the fact that the *Catechesis Celtica* (apparently of Irish origin) develops Orosius' three portents into ten. Despite all this, as Vernam Hull (art. cit. p. 26) has noted, none of Orosius' portents (with the possible exception of the second) bears the least resemblance to the miracles enumerated in the Irish text. Furthermore, for Orosius these portents take place in Rome, not at Jerusalem. These observations apply also to the expanded version of them in the *Catechesis Celtica*.

Thus, the history behind the Irish text still remains to be disclosed.

11A. ADDITIONAL RELATED TEXT

Text of British Library MS Egerton 92, f 28va

See Brian Ó Cuív, "The seventeen wonders", pp. 117, 124.

12. THE MAGI

McNamara, no. 48;

Extract from Infancy narrative in *Leabhar Breac*, beginning p. 137a.

Previously edited and translated by E. Hogan, "Legends on the childhood of Christ" in *The Irish Nennius*, pp. 58-73.

For the Hiberno-Latin tradition see Robert E. McNally, "The Three Holy Kings in Early Irish Latin Writing", in *Kyriakon. Festschrift Johannes Quasten*, Münster (Westfalien), 1970, vol. 2, 667-690.

The first two paragraphs of this text were cited by Sedulius Scottus in his commentary on Matthew (B. Löfstedt, ed., in the series "Aus der

Geschichte der lateinischen Bibel", Freiburg im Br., 1989) as coming from "the Gospel which is entitled According to the Hebrews"; the citation already in B. Bischoff, *Sacris Erudiri* 6(1954),203f.= *Mittelalter-liche Studien* I, 216; in *Biblical Studies. The Medieval Irish Contribution*, ed. M.McNamara, Dublin, 1975, 83; texts in English translation in E. Hennecke, W. Schneemelcher, eds. (Eng. trans. by R.McL. Wilson), *New Testament Apocrypha* I,151. The Irish text of the *Leabhar Breac* evidently derives from a very early Latin text.

13. ANECDOTE CONCERNING THE MAGI

Extract from text of "The seventeen wonders" (No.11 above).

14. INFANCY GOSPEL OF THOMAS

National Library of Ireland MS G 50. Based on edition of text by James Carney, *The Poems of Blathmac*, (Irish Texts Society, Vol. XLVII, Dublin, 1964)

See also Stephen Gero, "The Infancy Gospel of Thomas. A Study of the Textual and Literary Problems", *Novum Testamentum* 13(1971), 46-80; J. Noret, "Pour une édition de l'Evangile de l'enfance selon Thomas", *Analecta Bollandiana* 90(1972), 412; G. Philippart, "Fragments palimpsestes latins du Vindobonensis 563 (Ve siècle?)", *Analecta Bollandiana* 90(1972), 391-411; M.McNamara, "Notes on the Irish Gospel of Thomas", *Irish Theological Quarterly* 38(1971), 42-46.

The title now commonly given to this work "The Infancy Gospel of Thomas" is a recent one. The word "Gospel" figures in none of the manuscripts. In most of them the work is also anonymous. Its ascription to Thomas is found only in secondary branches of the tradition. The history of the apocryphon still remains to be fully explored. The work is extant in Syriac, Georgian, Ethiopian, Greek,

Latin as well as in this Irish verse adaptation. The original language seems to have been Greek. The relation of the various witnesses to one another has yet to be worked out. Three Latin witnesses are known: the independent Latin text published by C. Tischendorf in *Evangelia apocrypha*, ed. altera, Leipzig, 1876; the Latin text forming part of the Latin Gospel of Pseudo-Matthew; finally the Latin fragments of the Vienna palimpsest, edited by Philippart in 1972. The Vienna fragments and the Pseudo-Matthew text belong to one tradition, while that published by Tischendorf to a distinct one. It is recognised that the history of the apocryphon in the Latin West is a complicated one.

The Irish text is in verse. Its relationship to the other texts of the apocryphon have been studied by James Carney and M. McNamara. Its position within the apocryphon's overall history still remains to be determined. While it is important as an early witness for the apocryphon in the West, the fact that it is in verse, with the implied freedom for the poet author, seems to minimise its utility as a source for textual transmission. Each episode had perforce to be brought within the compass of a limited number of lines. It appears to be far removed from the original composition. The full history of this apocryphon in its (Greek?) original and various translations is being examined by Juan Severin Voicu, whose opinions on the Irish text we eagerly await.

15. THE ABGAR LEGEND

McNamara no. 51;

Text of *Leabhar Breac*, 146c28-147a3, collated with version of Trinity College Dublin MS H 2 17. Previously edited by P. Considine, "Irish Versions of the Abgar Legend", *Celtica* 10 (1973), 237-57.

This contains the well-known apocryphal correspondence between Jesus and Abgar. This has been preserved for us through its inclusion by Eusebius of Caesarea in his *Ecclesiastical History* and was known in the West through the Latin translation of Rufinus. See further P. Considine and McNamara, op. cit.

16. LETTER OF JESUS ON SUNDAY OBSERVANCE

McNamara no.52;

Portion of text of *Leabhar Breac*, 202b25 - 203b50, collated with other manuscript copies. For account of text tradition, see previous edition by J. G. O'Keeffe, "Cáin Domnaig". *Ériu* 2 (1905), 189-214.

Inclusion of texts such as this among "Apocrypha" brings to a head the problems of defining exactly what one means by this term. This letter, originating from the heavenly Saviour Jesus Christ, rather than the Jesus of history, and this well after the New Testament period, is not included in such collections of New Testament Apocrypha as those of M. R. James or E. Hennecke-W. Schneemelcher. A review of *The Apocrypha in the Irish Church (Études Celtiques* 1978, 138) contains a note of Professor Henri-Irénée Marrou saying he does not quite understand why the notion of "Apocrypha" is extended to include a work such as this. It is, however, admissible in the broader understanding of the term accepted by the Association pour l'Étude de la Littérature Apocryphe Chrétienne, which among its list of apocryphal texts features: "Lettre du Christ tombée du ciel". It is also included in F. Stegmüller's list (*Repertorium Biblicum Medii Aevi*, I, Madrid, 1940, no. 148).

For more on this and Hiberno-Latin texts on Sunday observance, see McNamara, nos 52A, 52B, 52C.

17. THE MYSTICAL TREE

McNamara no. 64;

Text of Book of Lecan, 193, 183(174)v[370]b.l.20; previous edition by R. Thurneysen, "Der mystische Baum", *ZCP* 14(1923), 16-17.

The theme of the cosmic tree is found in the Bible, in Ezekiel 31:3-9 and Daniel 4:7ff. As W. Eichrodt notes in his comment on Ezek 31 (*Ezekiel. A Commentary*, London, 1970, 425): "It is perfectly clear that the magnificent tree, described in vv. 3-9, is not just an ordinary tree of unusually large dimensions, but is identical with the great world-tree, known not only to Mesopotamian religion as the Kishkanu tree in Eridu, and to Teutonic religion as the world ash-tree in the Edda, but also to the Vedas and the Upanishads in India, and playing an important part even in China and in the religion of the Arctic tribes" (with reference to M. Eliade, *Die Religionen und das Heilige*, 1954, chap. VIII, pp. 299ff.). Illustrative texts from the Upanishads on the cosmic tree are given by M. Eliade in *Patterns in Comparative Religion* (Cleveland and New York, Meridian Books, 1963), 273f. The idea is defined fairly formally in the Upanishads: the Universe is an inverted tree, burying its roots in the sky and spreading its branches over the whole earth. Eliade devotes a special section to this particular theme: "The Inverted Tree" (pp. 274-276). A Sabean tradition has it that Plato declared man to be a plant turned upside down, with roots stretching to heaven and branches to the earth. The same tradition is found in Hebrew esoteric teaching (the *Zohar*): "Now the Tree of Life extends from above downwards, and it is the Sun which illuminates all". It occurs in Dante (*Paradiso* xviii, 28ff.):"the tree whose life is from its top". It is found, too, in Federico Frezzi, a Florentine poet much influenced by Dante: "the most beautiful plant of Paradise ... whose roots are above, in heaven, whose branches grow towards earth".

The "legend" of which the Irish text speaks is presumably some Latin work in the tradition of the cosmic and inverted tree which writers such as Mircea Eliade have examined.

18. THE DEATH OF JOHN THE BAPTIST

McNamara no. 55;

Text from Yellow Book of Lecan, col. 849; transcribed by Kate Müller-Lisowski, *ZCP* 14 (1923), 145-53, collated with the *Leabhar Breac* text (see R. Atkinson, *Passions and Homilies*, lines 818-960).

The text here published is composite. The first part is on the martyr-dom of John the Baptist. The second part (par. 8-11) gives the account of the revelation of the whereabouts of John's head which was made long afterwards to two monks from the east. This legend is basically the same as that printed by the Bollandists in *Acta Sanctorum*, June, vol. 5; new ed., Paris and Rome, 1867, 615-17; earlier ed., June, vol. 4, 716ff.

The first part of the text is a combination of biblical and other evidence. There are Irish secular texts on the druid Mogh Ruith, who in Irish tradition was involved in the beheading of John. On these see McNamara, nos 56-57.

19 GOSPEL OF NICODEMUS

McNamara nos 58-59;

Extract from text of RIA MS 23 O 48 (*Liber Flavus Fergusiorum*), ii, 26b, collated with the corresponding text of MS 24 P 25.

See also G. C. O'Ceallaigh, "Dating the Commentaries of Nicodemus", *Harvard Theological Review* 56(1963), 21-58; H. C. Kim, *The Gospel of Nicodemus*, Toronto, 1973; reprint 1979.

The text here published in translation is but one of a number of Irish texts having to do with the passion, death, resurrection, ascension of Christ, and with the Harrowing of Hell. This Irish tradition needs to be studied within the larger history of apocryphal writings on these matters, particularly in the Latin Church of the West.

The Apocrypha in question were very popular and that known in more recent times as the *Acta* or *Gesta Pilati* has been transmitted to us in hundreds of manuscripts. In medieval times this was known as *Evangelium Nicodemi* or *Gesta Salvatoris*. The Latin manuscript evidence shows that it was also known under a number of other titles, e.g.

Passio Domini secundum Nicodemum, Tractatus secundum Nicodemum, Historia Nicodemi, Acta Christi Domini, Explanatio dominicae passionis, Epistola de Pilato et Iudeis, Epistola Beati Nicodemi. Several manuscripts, in fact, refer to it as *Evangelium Nazareorum*, a designation drawn probably from another work known only through its title and some fragments.

The medieval texts of the *Evangelium Nicodemi* generally include the narrative of Christ's Descent into Hell, often referred to as part II of this work. However, the earliest manuscript of the apocryphon (the Vienna palimpsest 563) omits it. In the Latin manuscripts the *Descensus* is rarely differentiated by heading or otherwise from the preceding sections.

Another important point is that the *Evangelium Nicodemi* is preserved in Medieval Latin manuscripts through several lines of transmission. Furthermore, there are prologues and epilogues which are present only in certain of these branches.

All these points must be borne in mind in a study of the Irish material, as any one of them may be significant in identifying the particular tradition to which a given Irish text belongs.

The *Leabhar Breac* text is headed in Latin: "Pasio Domini Nostri Jesu Christi"; that of 24 P 25, "Stair Nicomeid ar pais Crist". The *Liber Flavus Fergusiorum* text, here presented in translation, ends: "gurubi sdair nicomett ara pais cunuigi sin" ("thus far the History of Nicomedus on his Passion"). Behind this designation there must stand the *Historia Nicodemi* (with metathesis to Nicomedi) of some medieval texts.

20. TEXTS RELATING TO
THE BELOVED DISCIPLE

20A. EPISODES FROM THE LIFE OF JOHN, THE BELOVED DISCIPLE

20B. FRAGMENT OF AN APOCALYPSE, AND DEATH OF JOHN

McNamara, no. 83;

Text of RIA 23 0 48 (*Liber Flavus Fergusiorum*) i, ff 32va-33vb (text 20A); 32ra - 32v a (text 20B); transcribed (without translation) by G. Mac Niocaill, *Éigse* 8(1956[1957]), 248-253 (text 20B); *Éigse* 8(1956[1957]), 222-230 (text 20A).
See now E. Junod and J.-D. Kaestli, eds., *Acta Iohannis* (*Corpus Christianorum. Series Apocryphorum* 1-2), vol. I, *Praefatio-Textus*; II, *Textus alii, commentarius, indices*, Turnhout, 1983; I, 109-116 for *Liber Flavus* material.

These texts have been transcribed in reverse order in the manuscript. A colophon at the end of text 20B describes the work as a "Life of John the Beloved Disciple", in Irish commonly called *Eoin Bruinne*, "John of the Breast", because he reclined on Jesus' breast at the Last Supper (John 13:25). The colophon also says that this Life of John was translated from Latin into Irish by Uidhisdin Mac Raighin. He was a member of the Canons Regular of St Augustine of Holy Island of Lough Ree on the Shannon and died in 1405. Presumably the order of the texts was different in Mac Raighin's original translation. Our present texts may represent but portion of this Life of John.

The source of text 20A, par. 1-8 is the *Passio Iohannis* of Pseudo-Mellitus; par. 9-14 of 20A are closely related to a very old text of the *Acts of John* found in the Oxyrhynchus Papyrus no. 850; see discussion in Junod and Kaestli, I, 117-136; McNamara, op. cit.

20B, par. 1-9, contains an apocalyptic text. It begins imperfect, the opening section being lost. The source seems to be some otherwise unknown apocryphal apocalypse connected with John; see text no. 27, par. 1 of this collection and M.R. James, *The Apocryphal New Testament*,

p. 190 (the Bogomile "Book of John the Evangelist").

Text 20B, par. 10-18 on the burial and last moments of John are from the *Passio Iohannis* of Pseudo-Mellitus; see Junod and Kaestli, I, 110 and II, 764, n. 3, 827-832. Paragraph 20 of 20B seems dependent on Augustine's *Tractatus 124 in Iohannem*.

The Life of the Beloved Disciple as translated by Mac Raighin is evidently a composite work. What remains to be determined is whether this is due to Mac Raighin himself or to the author of the Latin composition he rendered into Irish.

21. THE ACTS OF PETER AND PAUL

McNamara no. 85;

Text of *Leabhar Breac* (with omission of homiletic exordium and peroratio), previously edited by R. Atkinson, *Passions and Homilies*, lines 1681-1911.
see R. A. Lipsius and M. Bonnet, *Acta Apocryphorum Apocrypha*, vol. 1, Leipzig, 1891; reprint, Darmstadt, 1959, 119-177.

The *Leabhar Breac* text here presented in translation is thus introduced at the end of the peroratio: "Paul was imprisoned in the end, and was scourged by the Jews in Jerusalem, and was brought to Rome in chains to be exhibited before Nero Caesar, as is narrated by Marcellus, the disciple of the Apostles: - After Paul reached Rome...". Marcellus is a person mentioned in the original apocryphal Acts of Peter. The later composition *The Acts of Peter and Paul*, or *The Martyrdom of Peter and Paul* attributed to him was probably written in the sixth century. There are two recensions of this work. The longer begins: *Cum venisset Paulis Romam, convenerunt ad eum omnes Judaei dicentes: Nostram fidem, in qua natus es, defende* (ed. Lipsius, p. 191). The *incipit* of the Irish text corresponds to this and in point of fact this text appears to go along very closely with the longer recension, as edited by Lipsius. Determination of the precise nature of the relationship requires further study.

22. THE PASSION OF THE APOSTLE PHILIP

McNamara, no. 93;

Text of *Leabhar Breac*, 179b-180b; previously edited by R. Atkinson, *Passions and Homilies*, lines 2484-2570.

The text of *The Passion of the Apostle Philip* transmitted through Irish sources is quite different from the traditionally known "Acts of Philip". The Irish material agrees rather closely, however, with the entry for Philip in the *Apostolic History* of Pseudo-Abdias, where, however, no mention is made of his martyrdom.

Two features peculiar to the Irish texts seem to be the references to his tongue being cut out and his burial in Bethsaida. The legend regarding his tongue being cut out and restored gave Philip the name "The Evernew Tongue" in Irish tradition. See below, no. 23.

23. THE EVERNEW TONGUE

McNamara, no. 94;

Text of the Book of Lismore, 88a1-94c10. Selections; numbered specially for this edition.
Previous edition by Whitley Stokes, "The Evernew Tongue", *Ériu* 2(1905), 96-147.

There are three recensions of this work; that translated here is the First Recension. This is probably from the tenth century.

Opinions differ as to the nature of the work and the sources used. Robin Flower (*Catalogue of Irish Manuscripts in the British Museum*, 2, London, 1926, 557) thinks it probably represents a translation or adaptation of a lost Latin *Apocalypse of Philip*; the fragments of Latin embedded in the Irish text seem to point to a Latin source. M. R. James

(*JThS* 20, 1919, 9-13) suggests that the author has borrowed in part from Lapidaries and Bestiaries of the Middle Ages, and is also of the opinion that the text follows the Greek, as against the Latin *Acts of Philip*, in the record of the Saint's martyrdom. More recently, Peter Kitson ("The Jewels and Bird *Hiruath* of the 'Ever-New Tongue'", *Ériu* 35, 1984, 113-136) has studied the texts of the apocryphon concerning four magical jewels declared to possess a mystic likeness to human beings (par. 43-47 of Recension I) and concerning the monstrous bird *hiruath* (par. 58 of Recension I), and examines the presumed sources in lapidary texts and travellers' tales. He also notes the existence of the same traditions in the Latin MS BL Royal 6.A.xi (f 146v), a fourteenth-century text, and regards this Latin text as a hitherto unrecognized derivative of the Irish passages in question.

Much painstaking literary and source analysis is required before any really informed judgement can be passed on this interesting composition. Par. 58 has a tradition of the exotic bird *hiruath* (*hirodius* of Ps 103:17) which in substance is found already in the Hiberno-Latin commentary on this psalm in Codex Pal. Lat. 68; (ed. M.McNamara, *Glossa in Psalmos. Gloss on the Psalms of Codex Vaticanus Palatino-Latinus 68*, Studi e Testi 310, Vatican Library, 1986, 213); see M. McNamara in *Ériu* 39(1988), 87-94. The cosmological or cosmographical views of the texts should now be compared with such newly-identified commentaries on the Creation Narratives of Genesis; they will be found to have much in common; see M. McNamara, "Celtic Christianity, Creation and Apocalypse, Christ and Antichrist", *Milltown Studies* no.23 (Spring 1989), 7, 12f. The work might conceivably be better described as a theological treatise than an apocryphon, even though in the climate of ideas with which we are dealing the differences between one and the other may not be too clearcut.

24. *TRANSITUS MARIAE*

McNamara no. 97;

Based on text of MS Royal Irish Academy 23 O 48 (*Liber Flavus*

Fergusiorum), ii, f 48(49)a-50(51)b, collated with version in Bodleian MS Laud Misc. 610. The present extract corresponds to pp. 28-55 of the edition of the Laud text by Charles Donahue, *The Testament of Mary: The Gaelic Version of the Dormitio Mariae* (New York, 1942).

See also St John D. Seymour, "Irish Versions of the *Transitus Mariae*", *JThS* 23(1922), 36-43; Michel van Esbroeck, "Les textes littéraires sur l'Assomption avant le Xe siècle", in François Bovon, ed., *Les Actes Apocryphes des Apotres*, Genève, 1981, 265-285; R. Willard, "The Testament of Mary. The Irish Account of the Death of the Virgin", *Recherches de théologie ancienne et médiévale* 9(1937), 341-364.

In this edition the paragraphs are numbered to facilitate reference to Willard's essay.

We have spoken above (pp. xivf., with notes, xxi) of the special importance of the Irish material (both Latin and vernacular) for a history of the apocryphal text on the Assumption of the Virgin. The text here translated from MS 23 0 48 belongs to a family represented also by the other Irish vernacular text, Laud Misc 610 and the Latin text in Trinity College, Dublin, MS F. 5. 3. In his study of the texts M. van Esbroeck assigns a date c. 700 to the form of the apocryphon found in both the vernacular Irish texts. He classes it in the "Palm of the Tree of Life" type (by reason of its inclusion of this tree), and in his "genealogical tree" has it descend from the fifth-century Syriac form of the work. From the Irish form of text would have descended the Latin form of the *Transitus* edited by A. Wilmart in *Analecta Reginensia* (Studi e Testi 59), Vatican, 1933, 323-362.

The *Transitus* apocryphon proper ends with par. 49 of the present translation. The remainder is quite a different apocryphon, the story of a visit to the Other-world; as R. Willard notes (pp. 361f.), in fact, the *Apocalypse of Paul* in a new guise. Already in 1922 St. John D. Seymour noted the close affiliations of the Irish text with the Syriac *Obsequies of the Holy Virgin*. Later research agreed with him. It is noteworthy in this regard that also in the Syriac *Obsequies* there is a presence of the *Apocalypse of Paul* (Willard, 363).

It remains for future research to further develop the significance of these relationships. It appears that the Irish author of *The Vision of Adomnán* (tenth-eleventh century) had before him this apocryphal work in the form in which we have it in Irish sources (see text 26, par. 3 of this collection).

25. IRISH TEXT OF *VISIO SANCTI PAULI*

McNamara no. 91A;

Text of MS RIA 25 P 25, pp. 68-80 (ff 37c-38c); See J.E. Caerwyn Williams, "Irish Translations of the Visio Sancti Pauli", *Éigse* 6(1960), 127-134.

The Irish texts represent Recension IV of the *Visio Sancti Pauli*, a recension transmitted by a number of manuscripts, and also in the spurious homily 100 of Bede (in *PL* 94, 501-502). The Irish text here presented in translation, in fact, follows this Pseudo-Bedan Homily very closely.

26. THE VISION OF ADOMNÁN

McNamara no.100;

Text of *Lebor na hUidre*, ff 27a-31b (lines 1939-2301).

See David Dumville, "Towards an Interpretation of *Fís Adamnán*", *Studia Celtica* 12-13(1977-8), 62-77; James Joseph Colwell, "Fís Adamnán. A comparative study, with introduction, text, and commentary based on the version of the Lebor na Huidre" (Unpublished Ph.D. dissertation, University of Edinburgh, 1952); C. S. Boswell, *An Irish Precursor of Dante. A study on the vision of heaven and hell ascribed to the eighth-century Irish Saint Adamnán*, London, 1908; Jane Stevenson, "Ascent through the Heavens, from Egypt to Ireland", *Cambridge Medieval Celtic Studies*

5(Summer, 1983), 21-35 (includes treatment of the Seven Heavens in *Fís Adomnáin*).

In the words of David Dumville (art. cit. p. 77) the tenth or eleventh-century author "has created in *Fís Adamnán* a minor masterpiece of medieval literature; his work stands head and shoulders above the other visions of the early and central Middle Ages. He was indeed a worthy *Irish Precursor of Dante*".

A treatment of the literary questions, of the MSS and of the author's sources can be seen in Dumville's study. As sources the author uses the seven heavens apocryphon, the versions of *Visio Pauli*, and the purgatorial theories of Gregory the Great. Together with this, as already noted, he uses the Irish Apocrypha *The Two Sorrows of the Kingdom of Heaven* (text no. 6 of this collection) and the Irish recension of the *Transitus Mariae* (text no. 24 above). Thus, even if in itself it cannot be described as an apocryphal work, it contains so much apocryphal material that it deserves study among the Apocrypha.

27. ANTICHRIST

McNamara no. 104J;

Text of Book of Lismore, f 110a30-110c20. Earlier translation by Douglas Hyde, "A Medieval Account of Antichrist", in R. S. Loomis, ed., *Medieval Studies in Memory of Gertrude Schoepperle Loomis* (Paris, 1927), pp. 391-39ĉ.

The Antichrist tradition in Ireland has been studied by Brian Ó Cuív, "Two Items from Irish Apocryphal Tradition", *Celtica* 10(1973), 87-113 (87-102: I. The Conception and Characteristics of Antichrist). Here he lists the various vernacular Irish texts, and publishes an Irish poem on the topic from the *Book of Uí Maine* and a MS in the National Library of Scotland. In so far as the poem is intelligible, Professor Ó Cuív notes that its Antichrist Story has the following elements: (1) Antichrist is the son of his own sister who conceives him when her father, a bishop in Jerusalem, lies with her on the Friday before Easter at the instigation of the devil; (2) in appearance Antichrist has a flat face with one eye; (3) he has miraculous powers: he can make gold out of grass and anise(?) and wine out of water, he can cause disease and can cure the sick, he can create a moon, sun and elements(?), he can do anything that Christ did on earth except restore people to life; (4) he has a thousand fair women in his company. B. Ó Cuív further notes that comparison with other Irish texts shows several correspondences.

It remains for future research to bring together the Irish vernacular and Hiberno-Latin evidence on Antichrist and to study this within the larger context of the tradition, particularly in the Latin Church. See also M. McNamara, "Celtic Christianity. Creation and Apocalypse, Christ and Antichrist", *Milltown Studies* no. 23 (Spring 1989), 26-30.

28. THE SEVEN JOURNEYS OF THE SOUL

Texts: Verse form, *Leabhar Breac*, p. 88; prose: NLI G I;

Previously edited by Máire Herbert in *Éigse* 17(1977), 4-6, 8.

As the introduction to the original edition states, the origin of the idea of the soul's seven days of freedom after death is obscure, and probably derives from some primitive tradition. The Persians believed that the soul stayed on earth for three days after death, while acquiring no new knowledge of the world during this time. M. R. James (*The Testament of Abraham*, Texts and Studies II, 2, Cambridge, 1906, 122) notes the presence of the belief that souls made a tour of the universe in the time between death and judgement in *2 Esdras, Pistis Sophia, Apocalypse of Zephaniah* and the *Spurious Homilies of Macarius*. It is also found in the *Visio Pauli*. However, in none of the texts mentioned is the soul's tour set out in the systematized fashion of the Irish texts. The latter are probably based on a Latin original, but none has been traced.

The *Leabhar Breac* text is ascribed to "Moelmoedóc mac Diarmada",

probably identical with the person of the same name slain in the battle
of Cenn Fuait in 917 according to the *Annals of Ulster*.

29. THE SIGNS BEFORE DOOMSDAY

McNamara no. 104B;

Text of *Saltair na Rann*, lines 8017-8336.
See St John D. Seymour, "The Signs of Doomsday in the Saltair na
Rann", *PRIA* 36C(1923), 154-160; William W. Heist, *The Fifteen Signs
before Doomsday*, East Lansing, 1952.

This text is but one of the exceptionally rich Irish literature on the Signs
before Doomsday. On this see the summary in McNamara, no. 104.
The *Saltair*, dependent on the *Apocalypse of Thomas*, has the older Seven
Signs type, but spreads the signs over nine days and adds some new
signs. St John D. Seymour attached particular importance to the *Saltair
na Rann* text in the history of the development of the tradition in the
West, "in that it seems to serve as a connecting link in subject, and perhaps in time also, between the seven-sign group and the fifteen-sign
group". William W. Heist concurs with Seymour's view. In the conclu-
sion to his book on the subject (p. 193) he writes:

> I have tried here to show that the additional strophes, CLIII-CLXII,
> of the *Saltair na Rann* constitute a crucial text in the study of the
> origin and development of the legend of the Fifteen Signs before
> Doomsday. They are certainly the key to the study of the legend,
> and they are probably its actual original. For if the origin of the
> legend remains somewhat uncertain, it is only in the sense that we
> cannot prove beyond cavil that the immediate source from which it
> is developed was the matter in these additional strophes. The
> earliest clear trace of it appears here, and nothing in the legend
> points beyond these strophes to any earlier source, except to the
> recognized main source of *Saltair na Rann*, the *Apocalypse of Thomas*.
> But no other form of the *Apocalypse of Thomas* can dispute with
> *Saltair na Rann* the position of probable source of our legend. So it

is stating the case very moderately to say that it seems most likely that these strophes are the primary source of the Fifteen Signs, with *The Evernew Tongue* serving as the most important secondary source, even though we cannot quite exclude the possibility that the legend had been already formed when the *Saltair na Rann* was composed and that the latter borrowed from the legend as well as from the *Apocalypse of Thomas*, upon which it is primarily based.

This and a number of other contentions regarding Irish Apocrypha will, undoubtedly, undergo scrutiny in the current resurgence of scholarly interest in New Testament Apocrypha.

INDEXES

(References to text numbers and subdivisions)

26:2,42

Pharaoh(s), 9:3; 6:6

Philip (the judge), 18:1,2

Philip, son of Antipater, 18:1-4

Philip, son of Gordian, 26:42

Philip the apostle, 22, passim; 23:9

Pilate, 19,prologue, I-XII, passim

Roman(s), 10:1,5; 19,prologue; 21:16,18; 22:1; 26:42

Sailusa, 18:5

Samuel, 19:II,4

Satan, 8:6; 19:XX,1-3; XXIII,3

Satanus, 19:XX,1,2; XXI,1,3; XXIII,1-3

Sem[en]a (name of whale), 11:17

Seth 19:XIX

Seusisp, 20A:9-11

Silvester, 26:42

Simeon (of the Temple), 19:XVI,2; XVIII,4,5

Simeon, son of Joseph, 10:1-3,7,8,12,13,17; 12:1,3,10,12, 13

Simeon (father of Carinus), 19:XVII,3

Simon Cannaneus, 15:1

Simon Judas Iscariot, 15:1

Simon Magus, 21:2,4-15

Simon Peter, 15:1

Sirus, 19:I,1

Solomon, 7:7; 8:1

Tetos, 19:II,4

Thaddaeus the apostle, 15:1

Thaddaeus the disciple, 15:1,2,4-7

Thaddaeus (Judas Thaddaeus), 15:1

Thomas 20B:15

Thomas the apostle, 15:2,4

Thomas (Judas Thomas), 15:1

Tiberius Caesar, 19, prologue

Tinne (grandfather of Adomnan), 26:3

Tobias, 15:5,6

Virgin Mary, 16:12b; 20A,1; 17:2; 24:3; 26:6; 29:33

Zacharias (father of John), 18:4

Zacharias (the scholar), 14:22,23,29

Zebedee, 15:1; 16:12r

Zeno, 14:43

2. PLACES

Abuad, 23:39

Africa, 23:39

Agore, 2:3

agro (in agro Damasgo),2:4

Anathoth, 9:3

Anatole, 2:3

Arabia, 11A:1; 12:3; 13:1

Arabian (gold), 12:8

Archon, 2:3

Ardargas, 18:1

Arimathaea, 19:XI,3; XII,2; XV,1; XVII,1,2

Armenia, 15:2

Arton, 2:3

Ascolon, 18:2

3. LATIN WORDS AND PHRASES

4. THINGS